TRY NOT TO SUCK

The Exceptional, Extraordinary Baseball Life of Joe Maddon

Bill Chastain
and Jesse Rogers

TRIUMPH
BOOKS

Library of Congress Cataloging-in-Publication Data

Names: Chastain, Bill, author. | Rogers, Jesse, author.
Title: Try not to suck : the exceptional, extraordinary baseball life of Joe
    Maddon / Bill Chastain and Jesse Rogers.
Description: Chicago, Illinois : Triumph Books LLC, [2017]
Identifiers: LCCN 2017043272 | ISBN 9781629374765 (hardback)
Subjects: LCSH: Maddon, Joe, 1954– | Baseball managers—United
    States—Biography. | Chicago Cubs (Baseball team) | BISAC: SPORTS
    & RECREATION / Baseball / General. | TRAVEL / United States /
    Midwest / East North Central (IL, IN, MI, OH, WI).
Classification: LCC GV865.M232 C53 2017 | DDC 796.357092 [B]
    —dc23 LC record available at https://lccn.loc.gov/2017043272

This book is available in quantity at special discounts for your group or organization. For further information, contact:

Triumph Books LLC
814 North Franklin Street
Chicago, Illinois 60610
(312) 337–0747
www.triumphbooks.com

Printed in U.S.A.
ISBN: 978-1-62937-476-5
Design by Amy Carter
Page production by Patricia Frey

All photos are courtesy of AP Images unless otherwise noted.

To Patti, Carly, and Kel
—Bill Chastain

To my kids, Nate, Carly, and Emily
—Jesse Rogers

Contents

Foreword

Joe Maddon has had a profound effect on my life and career as a baseball player. I played for him in Tampa Bay then joined him in Chicago the year after he became the manager of the Cubs. He's always been a huge advocate of mine. I always felt, from early on, that I owed a lot to him professionally, at the major league level, because of his belief in me as a player, and his ability to communicate that to me when I was young. I needed that. I remember, after two weeks, being in the major leagues and struggling at this level, and trying to figure out if I really did belong here. He told me, "I just want you to relax, man. You're going to be a great major league player." He said, "Mark my words, you're going to play in this league for at least 10 years."

I remember him saying that. I remember exactly where we were. We were out in the infield in Oakland, we were playing the Athletics that series. It was my first road trip with the team and I started off 1-for-13. I just started off really slow offensively, just trying to figure out how to hit major league pitching. And when he said that, I remember thinking to myself, *He's crazy. How can he say that? He's just pumping me full of whatever. He can't really know that.* But he saw something in me that I didn't even see in myself back then, when I was just two weeks into the league. He saw something in my work ethic, in the way that I approached the game, in my abilities and my talents. And he saw the intangibles in me. He really watered that seed regarding my talent and ability at the major league level.

At this level, so many times you kind of assume, *Alright, a guy is who he is. He's going to either figure it out or not—it's up to him.* But it was important to him—even from his first year in Tampa Bay—to create an environment that fostered that growth as a player. It was perfect timing to experience that, and be a part of that growth. It's one thing that makes Joe so special.

Before I came to Chicago, Joe made a very, very strong pitch to me. I played for him and had some good years under him in Tampa Bay, and he always said incredibly nice things about me in the media. I always did the same about him, but you never know how that's going to change when you go somewhere else. All of a sudden, someone goes somewhere else and he's got another team and I'm playing against him, and things change.

But Joe's rhetoric and tone about me never changed, even after I wasn't playing for him. Even to the point where, when I was with Kansas City in 2015 and I was coming up on free agency, we played a one game make-up in Chicago, and he and bench coach Davey Martinez both came up to me and made their pitch. Basically, "You would love it here. You'd be perfect for this group of guys. This would be an unbelievable place to play. Every day, it's just unbelievable."

That means a lot, just them making their pitch, trying to get me to feel wanted, to be with him again, even as an older player, to mix in with this group of younger players. They've seen me at every stage. Joe's seen me as a rookie, he's seen me as I blossomed in my career, as I became an All-Star, and then as I became a free agent and did things on other teams. And, being a veteran now, he's always believed in me. That's all you need to know about that relationship. If there's one thing as a player you would want to know, it's that your manager believes in you. Joe showed me that time and again.

So, knowing that Joe was here, and knowing how he was able to get the most out of young players, including myself back in Tampa Bay, and also knowing his personality, knowing how he makes it a fun environment to work in every day, and how he tries to take pressure off of players, I knew that he was going to do great in Chicago. I knew that I wanted to be around that again.

The other thing for me was that we didn't ultimately get to accomplish what we wanted to in Tampa Bay, which was winning a championship there. And when he went to Chicago, and I had won one in Kansas City, at that point knowing that Joe was there just made it absolutely feel like icing on the cake. Not only if I could win this championship in Chicago—it hasn't been done in 108 years—but to do it with my manager and bench coach, when we'd worked together for so many years down in Tampa Bay, it was like, that would just be the ultimate career accomplishment. It was just something that I really, really wanted to do. So I signed and we won it my first year.

That's what Joe Maddon means to me, but I also think he's had a real impact on baseball. He really represents a transition in the game when it comes to the manager's role. When he showed up in 2006, managers were still pretty traditional in the way they approached players and the culture created in the clubhouse, especially young players. He came in right away and said we're going to be different. He came in and made his own mark in the game. I think once Tampa Bay started rolling, and we started to make a dent in that division—which was such a powerhouse—his ways kind of got everyone's attention, especially his philosophies and things he was doing to get a lot out of such a young team. I was a part of that. I saw it. Just like later, in Chicago.

Now you see some of the newer managers in the game are a lot more open to changing the culture in the clubhouse and not staying so stuck in the rigid rules, letting players flourish and be themselves. Since the time Joe Maddon showed up, he was the guy that wanted to make everyone feel comfortable and become the best version of themselves. That's a philosophy in his own life he carries, but he wants everyone around him to feel the same way. In this book you'll learn how Maddon became who he is and how, together, along with the rest of the Cubs organization, we broke the longest championship drought in pro sports history. The Hall of Fame generally hinges more on numbers than anything, but if Joe Maddon has the numbers then he's a slam dunk because of the impact he's made in the game of baseball.

—Ben Zobrist

1

The Hat

ONE THOUGHT ENTERED JOE MADDON'S MIND WHEN CHICAGO Cubs MVP third baseman Kris Bryant threw the ball across the diamond to All-Star first baseman Anthony Rizzo for the final out in Game 7 of the 2016 World Series.

Just one thought.

"One hundred eight," Maddon said months later during the team's next spring training. "Just 108."

One hundred eight represented the years between championships for the formerly hapless Cubs. It was the longest championship drought in professional sports history; the "Holy Grail of championships," people would call it. Like the chalice itself, a World Series victory from the longtime team from the North Side of Chicago seemed impossible to come by.

But Maddon led a revival culminating in this Game 7 win. A victory he would actually have to answer critical questions about later because it nearly slipped away from him. Rain, of all things, may have saved Maddon from a torrent of criticism potentially unmatched in baseball history. The one thing that all fans of the game dislike equally turned into the Cubs' savior: rain. Not long after the Cleveland Indians tied Game 7 at 7–7, the sky opened, forcing Maddon's team to regroup.

He did as well.

"I'm walking down into the clubhouse and I see the players veer off to the right," Maddon recalled. "I go up to my office and

I wanted to see the weather map. And I see my bag right there. And I'm like, *It's time for my dad.* So I look at the weather map and then after that I grab my dad's hat and stuff it down the back of my pants underneath my hoodie and I said to myself, 'Let's go.' I took him back out there with me and during the course of that next inning I kept touching it back there."

Maddon needed some magic after a series of decisions had gone against him. He chose his dad's Los Angeles Angels hat, the same one he had with him when that team won a World Series in 2002. Maddon was just a coach then, still a few years away from getting his own team to run for the first time. When things are going against you in baseball, people will try anything. Pray to the baseball gods, have a meeting, or just grab a hat.

"My dad was there when we won the World Series in 2002, same hat," Maddon said. "I had it under some books in my office facing the field and I went up and grabbed it. There's two World Series victories. He's been in the dugout for both of them."

While Maddon was playing weather man and grabbing his good luck charm, his players were meeting in a nearby weight room. That meeting became instantly legendary, as before the rain fell in Game 7, the Cubs were on the verge of yet another historic collapse. Right-fielder Jason Heyward led the talk, helping to calm an emotional group. Closer Aroldis Chapman was in tears and there were questions—similar to the ones Maddon would face later—as to how things had slipped away.

A near bystander in those moments, one who could barely speak or understand the language and wasn't even on the playoff roster, understood the importance of that meeting. Japanese infielder Munenori Kawasaki said the memory of that moment is seared in his mind forever.

"My favorite moment is the last game, raining outside and all of us meeting inside," Kawasaki said, "J-Hey [Heyward] talking, Kris [Bryant] talking, Anthony [Rizzo] talking." Kawasaki put his hands together. "I knew 100 percent we were going to win. We came together. Yes. 100 percent. We were together. J-Hey was talking. Chappy [Aroldis Chapman] crying. I don't understand English but I knew 100 percent we were going to win. That's my No. 1 memory."

Kawasaki may have known it but few others could have said the same. Certainly not anyone who's followed the Cubs over the years. "Loveable Losers" wasn't just a nickname, it was a way of life for them and 108 years without a championship was on the verge of turning into 109. Leading the Indians 5–1 and then 6–3, Cleveland had stormed back to tie the game behind Rajai Davis' eighth-inning home run. Somehow, Chapman got through the ninth inning unscathed and then the rain came, seemingly stopping Cleveland's momentum. When play resumed, the Cubs had a new confidence about them, while their manager had his lucky hat shoved down the back of his pants.

"I kept feeling it back there," Maddon said. "I was always aware it was there."

The Cubs took their final lead of 2017 in that 10th inning, then almost gave it back again in the bottom half. But for once in over a century things actually did work out for them. When Bryant threw the ball to Rizzo, every person associated with that team became a legend in Chicago. The man who was hired in 2014 for this exact purpose would achieve a dream that began in 1979 as a coach, four years after making it to professional baseball as a player, but one who never saw the major leagues.

While earning a ring with those Angels in 2002, and then getting a taste of the World Series as manager of the Tampa Bay Rays in 2008, Maddon finally found his Holy Grail. It's a championship arguably more meaningful to its fan base than any other achieved before it. That's why Maddon's mind wandered to where it did as Rizzo closed the glove on that last out.

"My first thought was 108," Maddon continued. "Then my family. And then I thought about the coaches. Having been a coach and not making even the minimum salary that a player makes, which I think is absurd. I thought about them and how it impacts their family. And clubhouse guys and trainers and everyone who works here.

"I went through that in 2002; it was a year of [labor] negotiations. There was no licensing. My dad was passing away, I was going through a divorce and my daughter was getting married. Really tough year. We won the World Series and that helped everything."

His 2016 win helped a lot of people as well, within the organization and outside. It would cement his legacy in a city he had only called home for a couple of years, though his accomplishments there would last a lifetime. A lifetime in baseball had reached its pinnacle for Joseph John Maddon.

2

Pino Maddonini

HELLO, THIS IS PINO MADDONINI....

Such is the greeting callers get when they are forwarded to Joe Maddon's voicemail. Delivered with an Italian accent, the message conveys Maddon's sense of humor and typifies how proud he is of his family heritage, as well as his hometown of Hazleton, Pennsylvania.

"It's a great place to be from," Maddon told *The* (Wilkes-Barre, Pennsylvania) *Times Leader.* "If you took all of the cars off the street, you would never know what year it was. It's a great small-town city."

Maddon's grandfather, Carmen, arrived in Hazleton from Italy bearing the name Maddoninni. Eventually the name got Americanized to "Maddon" to fit in with the wealth of Irish coalminers in the north-central Pennsylvania city approximately 95 miles from Philadelphia.

Carmen pursued the American dream, opening a heating and plumbing business in the 1930s. The business created opportunities for his five sons, who all worked at C. Maddon and Sons Plumbing. One of those sons, Joseph Anthony Maddon, would serve in World War II and fall in love with a Polish spitfire named Albina Klocek. Joe and Albina—"Beanie," as she was known—were married and lived in one of the four tiny, family apartments on East 11th Street above C. Maddon and Sons Plumbing.

The couple had three children, Carmine, Mark, and Joseph John Maddon, their oldest, who was born on February 8, 1954. He stood out early. Not only did he have athletic ability, he had a natural curiosity. Those around him recognized him as the kid who always wanted to know why.

Hazleton served as the ideal backdrop for Joe and Beanie to raise their kids.

A typical day would see Beanie cook Joseph Sr. breakfast. He would then leave the house to begin his work day at seven in the morning. Furnaces that weren't heating and pipes that had burst never adhered to regular working hours, so he'd continue to work until the phone quit ringing, the smell of his Phillies Cheroot cigar lingering behind him. Beanie had dinner on the table when he returned home.

"Dad wasn't a hugger or a kisser; he just smiled," Joe said. "He'd shake your hand and give you a big smile. He never missed work and refused to get sick. Always in a good mood. A unique man, who just had this way about him.

"A lot of people would have been miserable from time to time doing what he did. Dad never was like that. I think that's one of the reasons why everybody liked him. He'd always be in a good mood, and he was fun to be around. Dad had a modicum of consistency, was patient and kind. I know I've got some of my father in me, I've just never been as stable as he was."

Childhood memories for Joe included watching the fights on *Gillette Cavalcade of Sports* with his father. Joseph Sr. would fry pepperoni and complement the dish with Cheez-Its. Joe would drink a Coke, and his father a beer, while they enjoyed the action.

Mostly, Joe remembered his father's good nature and how giving he was of his time. Even if he arrived home tired after another long day of work, he'd spend time with his kids. In the winter, they'd shoot baskets at a make-do goal inside the house. Once the weather warmed up, Joseph, Sr. would be showing off his hook shot at their outdoor rim, or he'd be out in the yard throwing batting practice or playing catch.

Beanie resided at the opposite end of the spectrum from her husband. She doled out the discipline and could be more volatile. Beanie wielding a wooden spoon to Joe's hind parts wasn't unusual.

Like Joseph Sr., Beanie had an admirable work ethic, working at the Third Base Luncheonette around the block from the family plumbing business. The slogan for the family restaurant that specialized in cold-cut hoagies: "Next Best Place to Home."

Everybody in Hazleton seemed to be a relative and had something to do with Joe's upbringing, creating a halcyon, storybook climate. Cousins were like brothers and sisters. Aunts and uncles were like parents.

"Because I grew up in Hazleton and came from as large a family as I did, I got raised by more people than my parents," Joe said. "I knew if I got out of line around my uncle and my parents weren't around, I'd get smacked."

All the cousins went to school together and the families often gathered for meals and at the holidays. Beanie cooked many of those meals, and the family feasted on her marvelous blend of Polish and Italian cooking. Joe especially liked an

Italian cookie his mother always made around Christmas that had coconut inside.

It's a Wonderful Life remains Joe's favorite Christmas movie. The fictitious town of Bedford Falls reminds him of Hazleton.

Because Joe had so many cousins and friends, and a playground on the other side of the block—along with a playground inside the plumbing shop—he never lacked for someone to play sports or improvise games with. Like when they'd create a basketball rim out of a coat hanger, mount it to a door, and use rolled-up socks as the ball. Or they might venture to the Little League diamond up the street just past the cemeteries. Going deep and hitting the water tower lived as the goal. Local legend says Joe's drives found the target on many occasions.

Nobody had a lot of money—the Maddons certainly weren't rich, but the simplicity of life in Hazleton made for a truly wonderful life.

"Growing up in that environment, having an Italian father and a Polish mother, and going to school with nuns through the eighth grade, I definitely learned respect," Maddon said. "I think Hazleton built a toughness in me, too. When I messed up, I knew I had to pay for it if I didn't own it. Even though I wanted to take off in the other direction at times, I didn't. I knew better. I'm really thankful about those things, because that benefitted me in everything I did and would do.

"Really, I can't imagine a better place anywhere to grow up than Hazleton. People paid attention to you, so you always felt like they cared about you."

Major leaguers hailing from the Hazleton area included Norm Larker and Tom Matchick. Of course, Maddon and the others knew their names and what they'd done.

Larker had played for the Los Angeles Dodgers when they defeated the Chicago White Sox in the 1959 World Series. Matchick had played for the Tigers in the 1968 World Series when they defeated the St. Louis Cardinals.

Maddon and company dreamed of following in their footsteps. The fact that somebody from the area had made it to the major leagues made such a dream seem like a possibility.

Due to Hazleton's proximity to Philadelphia and New York, most of the residents of the city were fans of the Philadelphia Phillies and the New York Yankees. Leave it to eight-year-old Joe Maddon to be different.

When his father took him to Yankee Stadium for a White Sox–Yankees game in 1963, Joe decided to take another path. His father asked Joe if he wanted him to buy him a hat and, for some reason, the Cardinals hat captured him. Leaving the Bronx that night, Joe fashioned a navy Cardinals hat with a red "StL" stitched on the front. After that, he acquired an undying allegiance to the Cardinals.

He'd lay on the wooden floor at his home and listen to Cardinals games via a Channel Master radio, though keeping St. Louis' station KMOX radio brought a nightly battle trying to keep the station tuned and hopefully not losing the signal when the game was on the line.

"I had such a mental connection to the Cardinals," said Maddon, who would draw their insignia most anywhere out of his fierce loyalty to the team. "I had the privilege of listening to Harry Caray and Jack Buck. Through them I could see the Cardinals come to life at Sportsman's Park. Listening might have been more exciting than watching."

Maddon's favorite All-Star Game came in 1964, when the starting National League infield belonged to the Cardinals: Ken Boyer at third, Dick Groat at shortstop, Julian Javier at second base, and Bill White at first.

Phillies slugger Johnny Callison won the game with a ninth-inning home run at Shea Stadium, providing Maddon with a day he'd never forgot.

"Seeing all of the Cardinals' infield start that day was such a thrill. I just loved the Cardinals," Maddon said.

Like most kids of his generation, he initially watched the Midsummer Classic on a black-and-white TV. When his Uncle Jack bought an Olympia color TV, the game got better. Suddenly he could see the colors of every major league team gathered all at once.

"I watched most of them on a black and white, but when I got to see it in color, and the NBC peacock and all of that, it really brought everything to life," Maddon said.

In October 1964, the Cardinals met the Yankees in the World Series. The Cardinals claimed the Fall Classic in seven games. Even today, anybody could stop Maddon on the street and ask him about the 1964 Cardinals. He'd be able to spew out the team's lineup and rotation, highlighted by Bob Gibson.

From that baseball affiliation, Maddon also grew attached to the NFL's St. Louis Cardinals, which made him an admirer of quarterback Charley Johnson. When Maddon threw the football in the yard, he became Johnson throwing to Jackie Smith or Billy Gambrell. If he kicked a ball, he became Jim Bakken.

Maddon showed an ability to do things other kids couldn't do at an early age, like being able to throw a football 50 yards at the age of 11. Proper motivation and discipline came from his father and coaches. Maddon credited Ray Saul, his former Little League coach, along with Richie Rabbitz and Jack Seiwell, his midget football coaches when he was 10 years old, and later Hazleton High School coach Ed Morgan, for their efforts to give him a clear understanding about discipline.

"I also learned loyalty and trust," Maddon said. "We were all lucky to have been around caring men, who willingly gave their time for us. They all made sports more fun, and that made sports even more enticing to me."

Maddon led from his earliest days on the playground, or in any other game.

"Everybody bought into what Joe said," said Maddon's sister, Carmine Parlatore, in *The* (Allentown, Pennsylvania) *Morning Call.* "He was managing even then."

Maddon excelled in Little League, beginning as a nine-year-old. During his Little League pitching career, he lost just one game he started and that outcome came hand-delivered from his family. Cousin Frank "Bumba" Maddon homered off the water tank to seal the win. Joe maintained his level of excellence after Little League when he played Teeners Baseball (age 13 to 15), and that delivered him to the halls of Hazleton High School, where he starred for the Mountaineers.

During his junior season at Hazleton High, Maddon threw a no-hitter against Marian High in the Mountaineers' 11–0 win in the McGeehan League championship game. Employing, among other pitches, a quality knuckleball, he only faced 23 batters in the seven-inning game, striking out four and walking one in the game that took place at Tamaqua High School's field, giving the Mountaineers their sixth McGeehan League championship in the seven years.

"Joey knew what pitches to throw all of the time," Maddon's catcher, Mike Macejko, told the Hazleton *Standard-Speaker*. "There were times when I might have been calling something different, but he just knew what pitches to call. I just listened to Joey."

Maddon, who played shortstop when he wasn't pitching, later took the mound in the PIAA District 11 championship against a heavily favored Northampton High School after Hazleton coach Buddy Morgan went with his gut. Maddon was his guy. That feeling proved prophetic. Maddon came through. He struck out seven and didn't walk a batter. He also hit a three-run homer to give the Mountaineers a 4–1 win. There were no state playoffs at the time.

Maddon also starred on the football field at Hazleton High, where he started seven games at quarterback as a sophomore after his cousin, Ron Maddon, injured his leg. The starting quarterback was moved to fullback, and Joe was made the starting quarterback on a 5–6–1 team, completing 57 of 100 passes for 703 yards and seven touchdowns.

Maddon got tagged with the nickname "Broad Street Joe."

Part of that nickname originated from the fact Broad Street served as Downtown Hazleton's main drag. The other part of the equation came from the fact Joe Namath played quarterback for the New York Jets, and he owned the nickname "Broadway Joe." Namath also happened to be Maddon's favorite player.

"I was all about Namath. I wore white cleats, a full-cage face mask, the number 12, and even tried to throw like him," he said. "Everything Namath."

Maddon particularly liked the non-conformist in the outspoken Namath, who cut the figure of a playboy, grew a Fu Manchu, and wore a mink coat.

"I think that was something that was missing at that particular time, and I really thought I wanted to be that way, so eventually, maybe, I grew up to be a little bit more like that," Maddon told the *Tampa Tribune*. "But at the time [Namath] did do that it was very unique to society in general."

In his junior season, Maddon led the Mountaineers to a 6–5 season, completing 93 of 185 passes for 1,290 yards with 12 touchdowns. The team improved to 7–3–1 in Maddon's senior season. Due to an improved running game, he threw the ball fewer times, completing 54 passes in 109 attempts for 700 yards and eight touchdowns.

After three seasons, Maddon's tally showed 204 completions for 2,693 yards and 27 touchdowns, which established him as the most accomplished passer in the school's history at the time.

"He wasn't the most gifted athlete," Maddon's classmate Rick Rogers told *The* (Doylestown, Pennsylvania) *Intelligencer*. "He was just very smart, always thinking ahead. He was always the smartest guy. He knew how to play and he knew the game. He was a natural leader we knew we could always count on in the clutch."

Maddon's combination of intelligence and athleticism drew interest from Ivy League schools such as Princeton and Pennsylvania, then Lafayette assistant coach Joe Sarra showed up in Hazleton looking to sign a quarterback.

Sarra, who later coached at Penn State, carried the reputation of a guy who could not be outworked. He hung out at Maddon's locker and even get him out of class to shoot pool. Building up the high school senior proved to be his best recruiting tact. Sarra felt Maddon could be the finest quarterback to ever play at Lafayette College. He took out the Maddon family to dinner and might have sealed the deal with his habit of showing up at their doorstop bearing quarts of ice cream for Beanie.

Maddon opted to attend Lafayette on an athletic scholarship to play baseball and football.

The youngster wanted to go places, which could be a daunting task for a small-town kid afraid of change. Maddon later addressed that mentality in *The* (Easton) *Time-Express*: "Basically, the best piece of advice is don't let anybody tell you you can't do something, period. To be very honest, a lot of times in our area up there, people kind of shy away from getting out and trying certain things because they're concerned about failure. I think at times the support is not necessarily there to tell somebody, 'Go ahead and try it. Go try it. If you don't make it, that's fine.'

"I ran into a lot of opposition when I wanted to do different things back there. Fortunately, I was strong enough internally to try anyway, and I had the support from my family. But I've seen it work the other way, too. So don't let anybody tell you you can't do anything."

3

Joe College

JOE MADDON ARRIVED ON THE LAFAYETTE COLLEGE CAMPUS IN fall of 1972, eager to play football and baseball while expanding his mind studying economics.

Located in Easton Pennsylvania, Lafayette College is in the Lehigh Valley and overlooks the Delaware River. New York City is 70 miles east of Lafayette, Philadelphia is 60 miles south, and the Pocono Mountains are 35 miles north.

The school is known as a tradition-rich liberal arts college that today offers a bachelor of arts in 37 fields and a bachelor of science in 14 fields, including four in engineering. While the Lafayette campus sat approximately 60 miles from Hazleton, the place may as well have been the dark side of the moon for Maddon, who had spent his entire life in Hazleton's welcoming cocoon. After a couple of days on campus, he got homesick and called his mother, telling her he'd decided to come home to follow in his father's footsteps in the plumbing business. Beanie spoke frankly, telling Joe she wasn't about to endorse such a decision, and that he needed to take that option off the table. Joe obeyed Beanie's wishes. Soon classes started, as did football practice, and everything was fine.

Maddon became the quarterback on the freshmen team and wore No. 12. Neil Putnam was Lafayette's head football coach, while Steve Schnall coached the freshman team and the 5'11" Maddon.

Years later, Schnall called Maddon an early version of Doug Flutie, the magical Boston College quarterback who won the Heisman Trophy in 1984.

Schnall allowed Maddon to audible rather than demanding that he strictly adhere to the specific plays he called. In the 1970s, giving such freedom to the quarterback was unusual. Schnall did so because he trusted Maddon's intelligence, and because he had an ability to read what the defense was doing.

"Just by accident we were running RPOs [run-pass options]," Schnall told *ESPN the Magazine*. "We didn't call it 'RPO' in those days but we were checking from calling a pass to running the ball or calling a run and then he would check to a pass; things like that that nobody was doing, including the pros. This guy was way ahead of his time in terms of intellect and ability and great judgment. Great instincts in everything he did."

Schnall also instilled in his quarterback's mind the "ZD" philosophy, which stood for "zero defects" and dealt with doing things the right way the first time. That included creating a mistake-free culture that pursued excellence in every task and endeavor. Maddon credited Schnall for teaching him that philosophy, which he would embrace and use throughout his career.

During that freshman season, Maddon led the offense against Penn. George Azar coached Penn and had recruited Maddon to be a defensive back.

"I was really appalled by that thought," Maddon told *The Lafayette* magazine in a 2016 Q&A. "So we beat Penn [at Lafayette] and the moment the game was over I walked out to the middle of the field to shake [Azar's] hand; I made sure I saw him. I guess I was being somewhat of a jerk."

In the final game of Maddon's freshman season, he showed the stuff that would have made him a candidate to be the Leopards' varsity quarterback the following season. That performance came against Lehigh in "The Rivalry" game, and saw him throw for four touchdowns while completing 14-of-17 passes, including a stretch of 13 consecutive completions.

When Maddon ran off the field celebrating the win, he slapped hands with the team's kicker and dislocated his finger.

"That was the last football game that I played," Maddon said. "We beat them, had a really nice game, and that was the last time I wore football equipment and that was really cool."

Fast forward to the spring of 1973. Putnam was preparing for spring practice when Maddon visited him in his office to tell him he'd decided to pursue baseball and leave behind football.

Putnam told *ESPN the Magazine* that his "heart went down to my shoes."

"I'm behind the desk, and Joe's looking at me," Putnam said. "I said, 'Joe, have you thought this over?' And then I tried to obviously do a little bit of a sell job: 'We're looking forward to you coming into the varsity,' and, 'Great hopes for the future of the program,' and all the things a head coach would do.

"But in the end what I said was what I meant: 'If you've made a decision and you thought it out, then you go with your decision and with my blessing. You become the best baseball player possible and do it right. However, if you decide to come back, door's always open.'"

Maddon remembered making the drive home after making his decision. He had to tell his father, who loved football.

"I told my dad I didn't want to play football anymore," Maddon said. "That was the only time he was ever upset with me in our lives together. He stayed mad at me for about six weeks."

Maddon also called Putnam when he got home. He didn't want his coach to believe that he'd done something wrong that prompted him to quit the team. The bottom line was, he felt he had a better future in baseball and he didn't want to run the risk of getting hurt while playing football. In Maddon's mind, the decision was all about longevity and possibilities for his future.

Norm Gigon played professional baseball and reached the major leagues with the Cubs in 1967, hitting the only home run of his career off Juan Pizaro of the Pirates. He retired at the end of that season and took the job as Lafayette College's baseball coach. Maddon called him his biggest baseball influence. Part of that influence might have stemmed from a conversation when Gignon told him that the Lehigh football game of his senior year would be the last time he played.

In a 2008 article that appeared in the Allentown *Morning Call*, Gignon recalled that conversation.

"Joe had a strong drive to be a baseball player.... I told him the only way he had a chance [at pro ball] was to try catching," Gignon said. "I said, 'You have some skills and you have an outside chance to be a backup catcher if [the] other guy's a left-handed hitter.' I was very honest with him. I laid it on the table. He gave up football, and he developed into a very good college catcher.

"He wasn't a big kid, but he had intestinal fortitude and drive and a great balance on life. He was undersized as a quarterback and he was undersized as a catcher. He had a good arm, obviously was not very fast, and had good power, too. He was one of those tough Hazleton kids."

Maddon's teammate, Hal Kamine, played second base for the Leopards and told the *Tampa Tribune* that Maddon "was the stalwart leader of the team, even as an underclassman."

"He ran the pitching staff wonderfully," Kamine said. "He was a super defensive catcher. And boy, did he know the game. He was a real student of the game."

Maddon remained an avid Cardinals fan. When Lafayette traveled to Florida to play games over spring break in 1973, Maddon and the team were housed in a dorm at the University of Tampa. The Cardinals conducted their spring training in St. Petersburg, which put him in the proximity of his favorite team. That prompted him to hitchhike to St. Petersburg by himself to see the Cardinals play the Mets. He bought a ticket along the first-base line and found himself in Cardinals heaven.

"I had no idea where I was going, so it took me a while to get there," Maddon said. "After the game, I hitchhiked back to Tampa."

In 1975, prior to his senior year at Lafayette, Maddon played summer ball in Boulder, Colorado, on a collegiate team that won the National Baseball Congress championship in Wichita, Kansas. Teammates on that team included future major leaguers Joe Carter and Mark Langston. Maddon played well enough to entice the California Angels to offer him a contract.

"They offered me absolutely nothing," Maddon told the Allentown *Morning Call*. "I got zero bonus; I had an incentive bonus, which I never collected on.... There was no way I was coming back to school if I had a chance to play baseball. I wanted it that badly, and I was not to be denied."

Unlike early in his freshman year when Beanie told Joe he wasn't coming home, he got no resistance about leaving school. And a future in professional baseball had been born.

4

Coaching Calls

JOE MADDON DID EVERYTHING HE COULD TO SUCCEED AS A catcher in the California Angels' farm system.

Unfortunately, most of his duties were as a backup. Still, he embraced the life of a minor league ballplayer and everything that came with it, like cooking his own meals. No problem.

Meal money for minor league players could barely keep a rabbit alive, so teammates pooled their funds and got the catcher of Italian/Polish origin to whip up chicken, spaghetti and meatballs, and sausage and peppers. According to legend in the Angels' farm system, Maddon's marinara sauce could make a catcher's mitt edible.

Maddon's effort and desire were admirable. He worked hard, always volunteering to be the guy to come in and catch pitchers when the team had an off day.

Peter Ciccarelli, Maddon's manager at Single-A Salinas (California) Angels, told the *Tampa Bay Times* how Maddon responded to a visit from his father.

"Our starter got injured and Joe wound up in the lineup," Ciccarelli said. "He went 4-for-4 with four of the hardest line drives I've seen anywhere. Every time Joe would get a base hit, his dad would go around and introduce himself to the fans. 'That's my son. He just got a hit.'"

Maddon wasn't headed anywhere in the Angels' system. That lot in life didn't insulate him from competing against some of the greats, like Rickey Henderson.

"He was the last guy you wanted to see if you were trying to remain in an organization as a catcher," said Maddon, who recalled the experience of playing against the future Hall of Famer while in the California League in 1977. "He was very good. He was always ripped, and a strong runner. He was already a good player and I think he was only 18 and in his second year of pro ball. Man, he could run like the wind."

Maddon noted that Henderson stole 95 bases that season.

"He broke the Cal League in stolen bases while I was catching," Maddon said. "I think it had been 90-something at that time. I did throw him out once during that game and then he stole third and broke the record. [Henderson] was very funny. But you weren't laughing when he stepped into the batter's box. It was very uncomfortable when he got on base because you knew he was going to go. And if you had a pitchout or your pitcher was slow to the plate you had no chance."

Typical of Maddon, he remembered some color from that experience as well.

"That was back when Charlie Finley owned the A's and they were very lean in the minor leagues in regard to equipment," Maddon said. "They had to borrow our equipment. And everybody is coming up to the plate, they're borrowing my bat. And while I was catching the game, I'd see 'Maddon' on the bat and they were just beating the crap out of us."

Maddon identified a coming trend. Speed was becoming more of a prominent component to the game.

"There were a lot of guys who could fly back then," Maddon said. "I remember I had three catcher's interferences calls in one game in 1976 at Quad Cities. We were playing the Appleton Foxes (White Sox minor league affiliate). They had little Harry Chappas. And they could all run. I get three catcher's interferences because I'm coming out of the chute so fast. Because everybody was running back then."

When Maddon played for Quad Cities, he remembered Chuck Cottier being the manager and the frustrations they had trying to control the running game and receiving little help from the pitchers.

"Chuck would call a pitchout every now and then," Maddon said. "And every now and then it would be right for us. You didn't stopwatch it back then. There was no stopwatch utilization in the minor leagues in the '70s. We didn't do that. I just knew based on who my pitcher is whether I had a shot or not.

"But for the most part, there wasn't a lot of information for managers or coaches to catchers or pitchers trying to control the running game. You just held the ball, maybe threw over a couple of times. A quick step, a slide step, that wasn't really talked about back then. I didn't have a sign to give to the pitcher to say I want you to be quicker to the plate on this particular pitch. I don't know who was the first person to get into that."

Maddon would put further thought into how best a team could control the running game and he'd put that knowledge to use in the future.

Throughout his minor league playing career, Maddon received accolades for being the kind of guy who would make a great coach, instructor, or manager. He danced to a different beat, too. While the other players read the sports page or *The Sporting News*, he could be found reading *Rolling Stone* or books without pictures. According to minor league teammate Don Lyons, Maddon "had a plan for everything."

"We roomed together on the road," Lyons told the *Tampa Bay Times*. "We checked into this small motel, and we were getting ready to leave and I heard something plink into the ashtray. Joe had put a dime and a nickel in the ashtray. I asked, 'What are you doing that for?' He said, 'If I come back and either my dime or my nickel is gone, I'll know I can't trust them.'

"Toward the end of the year, he's still doing it. One day, we come back to the hotel and in the ashtray there's a dime and five pennies. Joe says, 'I think they're messing with my head! I've got to take a walk!'"

Unfortunately for Maddon, being colorful and having intelligence weren't prerequisites for reaching the major leagues.

Maddon did hit .294 for Single-A Quad Cities in 1976, his first season. But a broken hand robbed him of his power. Angels scout Lloyd Christopher ultimately delivered the verdict to Maddon, telling him he would likely be better served being a coach than a player.

In four minor league seasons, Maddon played for Quad Cities of the Midwest League, Salinas and Santa Clara of the California League, and the Santa Clara Padres, who did not have an affiliation. In 170 games, he hit .267 with five home runs and 69 RBIs, and never played above Single-A.

The Angels released him in 1979. The next year the organization came back to him and offered him a scouting job. By 1981, he had his first managerial post in the Angels' farm system managing a Pioneer League team in Idaho Falls. Maddon also married Bette Stanton in March of 1981, and the couple would have two children, Sarah and Joey.

In the summer of 1981, *Arthur*, *On Golden Pond*, and *Raiders of the Lost Ark* were playing at theaters, Luke and Laura got hitched on *General Hospital*, and Maddon reigned as the youngest manager in the Pioneer League at age 27. Holding said post, Maddon wore many hats for a club that played at McDermott Field, and averaged less than 1,000 fans a game. In addition to filling out the lineup and calling the shots, he served as the pitching coach, third-base coach, hitting coach, and he helped the Venezuelan kids with their English the best he could.

Rookie-level clubs like Idaho Falls could be difficult assignments for any manager due to the mix of players on the roster that included the more advanced—and older—college players, kids just out of high school, and Latin players struggling to adjust to a new country. Harmony wasn't a given.

Mark Bingham, a first baseman/outfielder on the team, got along well with Maddon. The manager was just four years older than Bingham, who had just graduated from Harvard University. Bingham recalled Maddon to *The Sporting News*.

"He was new to it," Bingham said. "I was already a college graduate. Some of the other players were younger. I remember one time he yelled at us for something. He pulled me aside after and asked, 'Did I sound tough?'"

From the beginning, he backed his players, and he received affirmation for taking that stance one time when the playing conditions of the field became an issue.

They had returned from an extended road trip, and when they showed up at McDermott Field, they found a place not befitting a professional baseball team. Maddon reacted to the situation by telling the team's general manager that the field needed to be fixed. The general manager wasn't about to be bossed around by a kid who wasn't even 30 and chose to disregard the request. Maddon returned fire by calling Mike Port, the Angels vice president. Shortly thereafter, help arrived to fix the field. Port stood behind the young manager because he had backed his players, the organization's greatest asset.

Idaho Falls had a young third baseman named Devon White, and Maddon would demonstrate his chops as an evaluator by hopping on board the train that felt White would best serve the organization as a center fielder. White went on to play 17 seasons in the major leagues and won seven Gold Gloves along the way.

Maddon managed Single-A Salem (Oregon) of the Northwest League from 1982 through 1983, and managed to find a little magic at Chemeketa Field in his first season, leading a young Angels team to a 34–36 season and a championship. He was voted manager of the year and he continued to grow.

Included in what he learned: taking chances isn't a sin.

Though such chances didn't always turn out in his favor. Like when Salem played at Eugene. They had runners on first and second with no outs when Maddon decided to roll the dice with chaos on his mind. He had the runners break with the pitch only to see a line drive turn into an inning-ending triple play. He filed that one away and often noted that he had not exercised that strategy since.

Maddon also did some amateur scouting while at Salem. Jack Howell was one of the players he scouted. After watching him, Maddon recommended the Angels sign him.

"I wasn't sure if I should've signed, but I went ahead and signed," Howell told the *Orange County Register*. "I'm doing great, there's only a month to go in the season and after two weeks, I blow my hamstring. And I'm thinking I've given up my senior year of college and now I probably won't get to go to Instructional League. I'm thinking it's over, I'm done, they're going to think this guy's hurt all the time."

Maddon quieted Howell's anxiety, telling him that he'd seen him play at Pima Junior College and at the University of Arizona, and reassured him that he thought a great deal of his ability. Maddon told Howell not to worry, that he'd be fine. He then convinced the powers that be that Howell should be included on the Angels' Instructional League roster, and he was.

Howell went on to play 11 seasons in the major leagues.

In 1984, the Angels assigned Maddon to manage Single-A Peoria, which introduced him to Steak 'n Shake. Late-night double cheeseburgers and fries washed down with a milk-shake became a staple—even though he was lactose intolerant. Peoria ranked as a favorite stop due to his relationship with Pete Vonachen, who had just bought the team and changed its name from the Suns to the Chiefs. They became fast friends, and Vonachen treated him accordingly, giving him a car to use, and even setting up a house for him to live in for the summer.

Maddon did whatever he could to help the team he managed by attending rotary, church, and chamber functions. Vonachen told the *Tampa Bay Times*, "We never ate so much Swiss steak at Methodist churches in our lives."

Illustrating Maddon's sense of humor, Vonachen recalled to the *Times* the following conversation that took place when Maddon was preparing for batting practice before a game.

MADDON: "Pete, you got any baseballs?"

VONACHEN: "Yeah, I got eight dozen, but they're for tonight's game…. Jesus, Joe, I'm sorry. I didn't think about ordering baseballs."

MADDON: "Well, Pete, they're essential for the game."

And even though Maddon's managerial career had just begun, he stayed true to his self. He wasn't demonstrative. Throwing objects and shouting at his players wasn't him, and that helped earn respect with the players. He also appreciated the fans, which he demonstrated on a nightly basis when he'd talk to them before the games, shaking their hands and signing autographs.

Maddon moved to Double-A Midland, Texas, in 1984, and he managed there for two seasons, where they played games in offensive ballparks that gave games a slow-pitch softball feel. That experience made him come to terms with his preference: he liked neutral fields and games slanted by pitching and defense.

Maddon's learning curve continued to grow, particularly in the way of things not to do.

Frustrated about Midland's losing ways, and especially miffed at the effort his club was putting forth, Maddon arrived early to the park with a bunch of classified sections from the local newspaper. He clipped out sections of the want ads and posted them throughout the clubhouse. Even the toilet stalls weren't off limits. Once the players shut the door and sat down to take care of business, they were greeted by ads for jobs other than baseball. The negativity ran counter against everything Maddon had ever stood for, and would stand for, and he admitted that he had been wrong.

Maddon's catching days, and what it taught him about trying to control the running game, prompted him to emphasize that aspect of the game, having his pitchers employ a "quick step"—which was what pitching instructor Marcel Lachemann called it.

"We didn't call it a slide step because we felt like that semantically was a better way to describe what we were trying to get done," Maddon said. "So I think during the early '80s was the first time I saw it come aboard. But even as a young manager I never really had all those signs for the catcher and relied on the catcher to call throw-overs. Trying to control the running game would become more intense."

Mark McLemore played for Maddon in Idaho Falls and for parts of two seasons at Midland, on teams that had little talent other than McLemore; White, who had changed to outfield by then; and Bob Kipper, who went on to pitch in the major leagues for eight seasons. Midland finished in last place in 1985 with a 59–77 record, and won just three more games the following season. Still, Maddon left an impression on McLemore, who played 19 seasons in the major leagues.

"Unbelievable manager," McLemore told the *Dallas Morning News*. "Very passionate about what he does, very knowledgeable. A great communicator. One of the things that makes him different is that he gets into the heads of his players and gets the best out of them."

The 1986 season proved to be Maddon's last as a minor league manager. He never experienced a winning season as a minor league manager, finishing with a 279–339 record. Still, the experience of managing those games stayed with him, even if the prospect of one day managing in the major leagues looked far away.

5

Moving up the Angels Chain

MADDON'S CAREER WITH THE ANGELS IS A WONDERFUL EXAMPLE of the lost process of apprenticeship.

He became the organization's roving hitting instructor from 1987 to 1993 and served as its coordinator of the Arizona Instructional League from 1984 to 1993. In 1994, he became the director of player development, while beginning his fourth season as the club's minor league field coordinator.

Bob Clear became a mentor to Maddon and played a huge role in Maddon's baseball education.

Maddon first met Clear when Clear was a coach and Maddon was still a player. Clear had not played in the major leagues or even managed there, but "Bob-a-loo" had coached in the Pirates' organization before joining the Angels in 1970. Former major league reliever Mark Clear was his nephew.

"He truly was the best teacher I ever knew," Maddon said. "His influence on me, really, was immeasurable. He impacted a lot of people, including me. I'm not sure I would have advanced the way I did without Bob Clear."

Among Clear's skills was an ability to evaluate talent, and being able to give players an unvarnished critique.

"Bob-a-loo wouldn't blow sunshine," Maddon said. "He'd tell them the truth about what they needed to do if they wanted to get better. Really, treated them like men. He taught everything better than anyone I ever met. And he could teach any part of the game. He was incredible."

When Maddon assumed the role of roving hitting instructor in 1987, Clear worked as a roving instructor for the organization, which often brought the two together, along with roving pitching coordinator Chuck Hernandez.

Clear cussed like a Marine and carried a rough demeanor. A Colorado native, he wore a shirt, jeans, and cowboy boots, and normally had a dip going. Old school all the way, Clear had an uncanny understanding of the game.

"Bob-a-loo was an old-timer, but he was definitely our mentor," said Hernandez, who has been the major league pitching coach for the Angels, Tampa Bay Devil Rays, Detroit Tigers, Miami Marlins, and currently, the Atlanta Braves. "He was our hero."

Maddon and Clear were kinsmen in a sense, and the perfect guy for someone like Maddon to serve his apprenticeship under.

"The thing about Bob-a-loo, you couldn't get any more grizzled, old school, tough minded—a seasoned pro," Hernandez said. "He knew everything about baseball. Not just pitching. He'd been a manager back in the day when you drove the bus, rubbed the pitcher's arm. He was a one-man show, right? So Bob-a-loo had a tremendous feel for baseball, the whole game.

"We would just snuggle right to his right arm. You wouldn't find a tougher, meaner, grizzled guy that the players, A) loved, and B) he wasn't opposed to looking at anything new or modern. A lot of times Joe would come up with some things he wanted to try… and the old guys would be rolling their eyes like, yeah, yeah. Bob wasn't that way."

Maddon credited Clear for challenging him daily, but not when he was a player, because the talent-shrewd Clear didn't view Maddon as a potential major leaguer, rather a prospective coach for the organization. When they talked baseball, they went back and forth with their various points, and both were willing listeners.

"He always wanted me to be the best that I could be," said Maddon, who allowed that Clear had told him he'd one day be a major league manager.

Troy Percival proved to be one player Maddon and Clear could not agree about regarding his future.

The Angels signed Percival as a catcher out of the University of California-Riverside, but he'd been a bust in his first season of professional baseball, hitting .203 with five RBIs in 79 at-bats for Boise in 1990.

Ever the keen eye for talent, Clear identified Percival's power arm. Contrasted to his lack of offense, Clear considered the prospect of moving Percival to the pitching mound a no-brainer.

"I loved Bob-a-loo," Percival said. "He told me I was the worst hitter that organization had ever seen and I needed to get on the mound. I had to agree. I couldn't hit anything—wasn't just trouble with breaking stuff."

Percival liked Clear's idea; Maddon did not, initially.

Percival said he'd known Maddon intimately "way longer than anyone else," dating back to his first year in the Angels' organization.

"He's always been so calm and able to discuss and explain things better than anybody I'd ever been around," Percival said. "He was right there when I changed from catcher to pitcher. He was right there in the middle of it."

Maddon thought the organization needed to let the situation play out a little further, noting that the scouts had seen something that attracted them to Percival, something that made them want to bring him into the fold as a catcher.

"Joe was against me turning into a pitcher at that time," Percival said. "He said, 'It might happen, but I think I can teach you to hit.' I looked at him straight in the eye and said, 'I don't think you can.'

"You know how many times I had to sit down with him when we went through the whole debacle of changing from catcher to pitcher, and sharing opinions. He's such a real human being and he always has been, and I think that's why he gets so much respect from his players. He is the real thing and it's not going to change."

Maddon got voted down, primarily due to Clear's influence, thus, he rolled with the punches accordingly.

"I was frustrated with it and Joe knew that," Percival said. "He said, 'I think you've made your choice and when you walk out of this office, you're not changing back.' That was probably one of the best things he could have said. Regardless of agreement or disagreement, there wasn't going to be any wavering on the decision. We were going to go after it full throttle."

On the mound, Percival had a simple, powerful delivery, and, in Clear's opinion, they needed to leave him as he was, even though it wasn't the most aesthetically pleasing delivery. Turned out, Clear was on point.

After four minor league seasons, Percival became Angels closer Lee Smith's set-up man in 1995, posting a 3–2 record with a 1.95 ERA in 62 games. The next season Percival became the Angels' closer and he would spend 14 seasons in the major leagues, notching 358 career saves.

Maddon might have been wrong about Percival, but he was right about plenty of others, including outfielder Tim Salmon.

Maddon went back a way with Salmon. He'd seen him play at Grand Canyon University before the Angels drafted him in the third round of the 1989 June Draft. All along he felt like the sturdy outfielder would be a guy the Angels could build a team around. When he struck out 166 times at Midland in 1991, Maddon went to bat for Salmon, even though more than one evaluator in the Angels' organization pushed for Salmon to play another season of Double-A ball. Maddon crunched the numbers and came up with a positive: Salmon had only struck out 62 times in the second half.

Riding Maddon's endorsement, Salmon moved up to Triple-A Edmonton in 1992 and hit .347 with 29 home runs and 105 RBIs. He lowered his strikeouts to 103, while walking 91 times and reaching the major leagues that season. Later Salmon—or "Fish" as Maddon called him—became a cornerstone of the Angels' offense.

Hernandez observed about Maddon that, "He gets people in general. And players respond to him because of his positive ways. Sometimes he'll tell you you're being positively stupid. He just has a way of handling that."

Ask Maddon about himself, and he'll always credit the Angels for having a "fantastic" organization, including the likes of Mike Port, Bill Bavasi, Terry Collins, Clear, Marcel Lacheman, Loyd Christopher, and Preston Gomez. But he called Gene Mauch "the god," noting that Mauch could see the simple things that people routinely overlooked, or missed completely.

"I've always described him as someone who was dripping with common sense," Maddon said.

Mauch played in the major leagues as a second baseman for six teams from 1944 through 1957, but he was more known for his days managing the Philadelphia Phillies, the Montreal Expos, the Minnesota Twins, and the Angels, which he managed from 1981 to 1982 and from 1985 through 1987.

Mauch's Phillies were running away with the National League pennant in 1964. Sluggers Johnny Callison and Richie Allen led the Phillies' offense, and starting pitchers Jim Bunning and Chris Short were the aces of the staff. Those were the days when there were no playoffs. The champions of the National and American leagues met in the World Series.

The Phillies were in first place with a 6½ game lead at 90–60 with just 12 games left to play as they headed into a seven-game homestand at Connie Mack Stadium. With a spent pitching staff, Mauch made the decision that would haunt him. He opted to pitch Bunning and Short in seven of the final 10 games—even though doing so required four of the starts to be made on two days' rest. The Phillies lost 10 in a row before winning their final two games. By then, all had been lost. The St. Louis Cardinals stormed to the pennant, winning nine of their final 11 games. They met the New York Yankees in the World Series and became world champions when they won in seven games.

Mauch got blistering reviews addressing how he'd managed his team down the stretch in '64. Still, most in baseball would have acknowledged, grudgingly, or otherwise, that Mauch had forgotten more baseball than most would ever know. Maddon understood that and sipped from that fountain of baseball knowledge whenever possible.

"He had an amazing ability to make complex things simple," Maddon said.

Ironically, one of Maddon's favorite childhood memories came at Mauch's expense since Maddon had been a 10-year-old Cardinals fan pulling for them to overtake Mauch's Phillies.

Mauch took over as the Angels manager prior to the 1981 season, which afforded Maddon the opportunity to get to know Mauch better while serving as a spring training "grunt" for the Angels in 1981 and 1982. Maddon would throw batting practice and catch pitchers, anything to be useful. Mauch often requested that Maddon threw to the team's better hitters, and he took care of Maddon for doing so.

When Maddon served as the Angels' coordinator of the Arizona Instructional League from 1984 to 1993, his baseball education under Mauch continued.

"He had a way of giving you little thoughts about all kinds of things, and they would stick," Maddon said. "We were at Instructional League and I was throwing batting practice. He told me, 'You've created a great atmosphere around here. I thanked him and kept throwing BP, but I didn't really know what he was talking about. Once I thought about it, I realized he was referring to organizational skills and relationship building. I was doing all these things outside peripheral things, but I didn't realize how important they were to getting things done. To this day, I consider it one of the greatest compliments I've received."

Maddon came to realize that Mauch's compliment dealt with trust.

"How to play baseball isn't rocket science," Maddon said. "People want to focus on the minutia of the game. But trust is a lot more important than whether you hit a cutoff man. Learning to trust each other is a lot more difficult.

"When you're trusted, guys will disagree with you instead of just agreeing with you because you're in charge. I came away understanding how powerful trust was."

Maddon especially loved to talk strategy with Mauch. For example, Mauch would grumble if one of his pitchers threw anything resembling a strike on an 0-2 count. And he loved first-pitch breaking balls, because he felt that could set up an at-bat that favored the pitcher.

"I can't tell you what kind of influence he had on me," Maddon said. "I never questioned anything he said, because I just knew it was right."

Maddon cited the fact that Mauch had been one of the first managers he knew that put deep thought into trying to control the running game.

"Gene was very much into controlling the running game and worried about pitchers' times to the plate," Maddon said.

Maddon found a different person in his relationship with Mauch than the prevailing perception of Mauch as a gruff person you wanted to avoid.

"He wasn't that way at all," Maddon said. "I'd go in his office and we'd talk about all kinds of things. I think he liked my sense of humor."

People listened to Mauch and usually jumped. He believed in *team*, and liked to play "small ball," or moving the runners along via sacrifice bunts and hitting behind the runner. Mauch brought wisdom and toughness to the equation, and was well respected.

In 1986, Mauch managed the Angels to the American League West title, and led the Boston Red Sox three games to one in the American League Championship Series. Holding the lead in the fifth game, Boston's Dave Henderson hit a home run off Angels reliever Donnie Moore to put the Red Sox ahead. The Angels managed to tie the game in the bottom of the ninth, but the Red Sox won the game in extra innings then won the final two games of the series in Boston to advance to the World Series.

Mauch retired his post as Angels manager in the spring of 1988, citing health reasons for his hasty departure.

Hernandez agreed with Mauch that Maddon indeed created a great work environment.

"Like when we used to run Instructional League with this really talented group of young players," Hernandez said. "He used to have a t-shirt: 'Every day counts.'

"Because we were out there in October and it's 106 degrees in Arizona, so who cares about you? The Angels just got done with the season. But in Joe's world, what we did that day was as important as anything that was happening on the planet. And he could make the kids feel that kind of way, too."

Maddon had a knack for teaching as well.

"I know he was a good hitting coach," Hernandez said. "I think he had a tremendous influence on many."

The archives are littered with success stories, like Ruben Amaro finding success after Maddon adjusted his stance by getting him to lower his hands. Outfielder Wiley Lee had hit only nine home runs in his first three professional seasons, but he hit three in two games after Maddon told him to start getting more aggressive. And when Devon White was striking out too much, Maddon helped him shorten his swing by using more hands and less arms.

Players in the Angels' organization revered Maddon and embraced him for the knowledge he passed on to them.

"My early years there, he was the minor league hitting rover," said Joey Urso, who played in the Angels' organization from 1992 through 1997. "He went from town to town to visit all of the organization's hitters. The communication he had with all of the hitters was really second to none. Just the way he communicated and related to the players.

"Hitting can become very mental, and he just had a way of communicating with you to free the mind. The different drills he would put you through to help you have success in the games is what I remember the most. When you're in the minors and you have rovers who come in, who only see you once a month or every six weeks, sometimes it can be really tough on hitters to be hearing another voice. And with him, it was totally the opposite. He just simplified things for you."

Urso marveled at how Maddon remembered each player given the number of players he saw.

"He had a way of making everyone feel special," Urso said. "That's his way. A guy that communicates that well and makes you feel like that, it's easy to trust them. When you're talking about hitting, it's a tough art. He gave you this sense of confidence at practice and in drills to get ready for that game, even in the short stints that he would visit each club, because these rovers would come in four or five days at a time and then you don't see them for five or six weeks. So it's tough for them to get their message across sometimes, and he was just outstanding about that."

Urso allowed that there were some roving instructors most players didn't want to see. In contrast, a visit from Maddon felt like going out for a beer with your favorite uncle.

"Some guys try to put their stamp on a hitter," Urso said. "Joe was all about getting you into a position to succeed. For me, hitting is so mental and he just freed your mind."

Urso went on to become the baseball coach at the University of Tampa. Of course, Maddon was more than willing to help him with his new job.

"When I was offered a coaching job, by then he was in the major leagues, and he took the time to give me a bunch of charts and different things coaches need to look for," Urso said. "Tendency charts against the opposing hitters, and aligning defenses that you learn as a coach, but I didn't expect it to come from a big league coach to a first-year guy getting started.

Just says a lot about what his personality is all about and how much he cares about others."

Gary DiSarcina first met Maddon when he served as the roving hitting instructor. He credited Maddon with being a positive influence on him when he needed it most.

"He taught me how to fail," DiSarcina said. "I'd never really struggled until 1990, when I played for Edmonton. I'd look forward to him coming by to work with me. Teaching me about all different kinds of things. We'd talk about hitting with two strikes or stuff outside of baseball. I ended up hitting .212 that season, but I felt like it was the most valuable year of my career since I learned how to fail. You're going to fail in baseball, and he taught me how to handle failure. Later in my career, I could always go back to what he taught me."

Based on Maddon's stellar work as the organization's roving hitting instructor, the Angels identified him as the top mentor in the organization. The designation jived with Angels manager Doug Rader's grandiose idea to shift the emphasis of the organization to building their major league club with players from their own farm system rather than spending on free agents. Accordingly, the Angels created a new title for Maddon prior to the 1991 season: coordinator of instruction. Under his new title, his responsibility was to oversee the entire Angels system. The job called for him to design a curriculum for the entire Angels' minor league system. In addition, he took care of player evaluation and assignment at every level.

Hernandez offered that he'd been in the game for a long time, and that he'd "been fortunate to be around some good people and some good guys.

"But one of the things Joe gets as good as anybody, or better than anybody I've seen, he gets the young guy," Hernandez said. "He gets the young player. He knows how to make them feel good about themselves. Very positive. Everyone tries to be positive, but when it really matters, he's still positive. He can still figure it out. It's not, 'What you did was wrong when I took you out of the game.' He wants to know how you feel about me taking you out of the game. That was always his art form.

"I always thought that Joe would be the best manager, yet I didn't know if he'd ever get a chance, because he didn't get to the big leagues as a player. Sometimes you're not anointed. I always felt if he got a chance, he'd crush it."

Hernandez remembered Maddon being forward thinking, or "thinking outside the box" before such a phrase even existed.

"He was using the computer way back in the day," Hernandez said. "Back when most baseball guys were like, 'We don't need that.' You're talking about the 1980s. Because he was forward thinking, we used to have more interesting guests than you could imagine."

For example, Maddon arranged to have Kevin McNair come around. He coached track at the University of California-Irvine and had coached renowned sprinter Houston McTear.

"Joe brings him in, nobody had done that," Hernandez said. "And nobody had ever brought in a running coach. And he's teaching our guys—Tim Salmon, Jim Edmonds, Garrett Anderson, and Gary DiSarcina—we had a good minor league group when we were in the minor leagues together. Bringing in McNair was like a unique thing.

"Hell, I learned some stuff, because we had the tradition back then that pitchers would run the lines. You'd run 30 poles [from foul pole to foul pole]. I asked the guy, 'Watch what we do.' And he said, 'I don't have to, I've already seen what you do. It's dumb. I don't see you doing that to their arms. Why do you do that to their legs? By August they're cooked.' So Joe would bring in a guy like that, or a guy who came in with tennis balls—red, blue, and green ones. And guys are hitting off him. Anything. Joe wasn't afraid to try anything or experiment with anything."

Orlando Palmeiro proved to be another of Maddon's experiments.

While at batting practice for Single-A Quad Cities, Maddon observed the young outfielder throwing with his right hand, giving Maddon cause for pause. Didn't Palmeiro throw with his left hand? He thought some more. He did throw with his left hand. But he looked like a right-hander when he threw.

Turned out, Palmeiro was ambidextrous. Being able to throw with either arm was something to put on display for teammates. But Maddon tucked the information away and let it percolate. Palmeiro's 5'11", 155 pounds would play better in the infield. What would happen if Palmeiro, the left-handed outfielder, tried to convert to a right-handed throwing infielder? After all, they liked him, but were concerned that his size might hold him back. Having the additional position flexibility might help him reach the majors. That led to an Instructional League invitation being extended to Palmeiro to see if such an experiment could work.

Once at Instructional League, Palmeiro delivered an interesting game when he started at second then changed to a left-handed outfielder's glove and played center field, throwing out two runs at the plate.

Palmeiro eventually made it to the major leagues as an outfielder, but seeing what he could do as an infielder certainly didn't hurt. Nothing explored, nothing gained.

Vance Lovelace pitched on the same Hillsborough High pitching staff in Tampa, Florida, that also included future major leaguers Dwight Gooden and Floyd Youmans. Standing 6'5", 205 pounds, Lovelace had a big fastball. Big enough to entice the Chicago Cubs to select the left-hander in the first round of the 1981 Draft. He never managed to harness his control, so he bounced around the minor leagues until he found himself in the Angels organization. Once amid the Halos, Lovelace got a firsthand look at Maddon.

"He was the field coordinator, very detailed and always wanted to get the pulse of the player," said Lovelace, who briefly reached the major leagues and has worked as a scout and front office executive for the Dodgers. "That's why I think he does a really good job, because he has an innate ability to connect with people."

Even back in the late 1980s, Lovelace could identify what Maddon had that other coaches did not.

"He had the ability to connect," Lovelace said. "He wasn't an authoritarian. A guy that was screaming and yelling. He could get his point across without all of that. Him being the field coordinator, it was like, he would just tell you like it is. I appreciated that. You appreciated that as a young man and you appreciate it even more when you get older.

"He could explain to you what you needed to do to get better. What was going to be expected of you. And you got the message. You didn't just walk away confused. It wasn't threatening, but you knew he was serious. For example, he told me I needed to get better in my overall position. Being consistent. Throwing the ball over more consistently. But it wasn't something he expounded on, because he let the pitching coaches and the other people do their jobs. It was a blunt assessment. But it wasn't like you walked out of the room and you were like, 'I don't like that guy.' You understood."

Per Lovelace, Maddon was "ahead of his time."

"Back then there was a lot of screaming and yelling, and coaches who were like, 'You do it my way, or the highway,'" Lovelace said. "He was talking millennially before it became the way to talk to guys. Now you have to talk to guys that way because they're so about me, me, me, and they just go into a shell when you criticize them. You almost have to coddle them. They need to know all the answers.

"Well, he was doing that back then when everything was stern. He was a different cat. And now it just kind of falls into line with the way society is today. He just had a good understanding of people. And most people coming up during that time, you were raised by some stern people. You liked it or you didn't, but you were raised by certain people and you had to have thick skin. A lot of people back then thought he was a different cat. But if you look at it now, he was before his time. He fits right in now. The bottom line is, he cares. He cares about people. But things have to get done, too. Don't mistake the kindness and the thought track for weakness. That's not even close."

Hernandez said Maddon "saw stuff that was ahead of our time at that time…. He was bright that way, a little bit anal, too," Hernandez said. "The schedule had to be perfect. Because back in those days that's what he did. Now he's more loose. But back then, everything was to a T.

"I remember walking into a stack of papers for a workout. We'd done these workouts for 10 years and we knew how to do them blindfolded. Thirteen papers stacked on top. So I'd come in just to annoy him and start ripping off every paper unless it said pitching on it—PFP, Field 3, or something like that. And he'd say, 'Charlie, that's good paper, you're wasting all of the papers.'"

Hernandez chuckled, stressing the fact that schedules for a workout can be drawn up quickly, citing former major league coach and manager Gene Lamont as an example.

"He used to write a schedule in the morning before we went out at spring training, and it was a good schedule," Hernandez said. "And we'd have a good workout. These days there's a lot more that goes into the thing. Now we've got kids who are hired to spend the whole winter writing up the schedule for spring training. It's not complicated. But Joe was very much into it."

Disdaining handwritten schedules, Maddon used a Panasonic word processor for the many schedules and notes he posted in clubhouses. Eventually, he put the Panasonic to rest and got an Intel 386. Though he had to literally lug around the computer

due to its size, Maddon had top-of-the-line technology at his fin-
gertips. That machine allowed him to create beautiful schedules
and to delve deeper into the world of statistical analysis, such as
where opposing hitters hit the ball on a regular basis, matchups,
and all the minutia that would later infiltrate the game. He also
tried to look beneath the surface to find things that might not be
quantified by standard statistics, but influenced the outcomes
of games. "Jug runs" was one of his favorites. Said runs were
basically add-on runs when a team had a lead. Scoring jug runs
allowed a team to put a game on ice.

Away from the field, Maddon's appetite for reading grew.
Mark Twain and James Michener became favorites. He called
Michener's *Centennial* the first significant book he read, after
his Uncle Chuck recommended it. From reading that book, he
latched on to how the Native Americans would navigate the
lead buffalo toward the cliff and how the rest would follow
him over the cliff to where the rest of the Indians waited for
them to fall so they could carve them up for food. The lesson
learned: any good administrator wants to latch on to the lead
buffalo and get him headed in the right direction, as the others
will follow.

Throughout Maddon's career, he remained positive about
his plight, even though he longed to be in the major leagues.
He did get upset with the organization during the early 1990s
when he thought he was in line for a major league coaching job
and didn't get it. Discouraged, he wasn't his normal enthusiastic self when he got on a flight to return to his job for another
season amid the minor leaguers. From that experience, he
learned a philosophy that he has embraced ever since.

A sour Maddon found himself sitting next to a woman who wanted to talk. He did not and, obviously, his mood reflected that sentiment. That's when the woman delivered gold, telling him that whatever he put out there was going to come back to him. The woman's words struck a chord. Maddon's resulting epiphany changed his attitude completely. He decided he would always try to appreciate where he was and would always try to make the best of where he was and what he was doing. If you're negative, you will receive negative in return. Conversely, a positive outlook will receive positive in return.

Better things were on the horizon for Joe Maddon.

6

To the Major Leagues

NEWTON'S THIRD LAW OF PHYSICS STATES THAT EVERY ACTION has an equal and opposite reaction. Thus, when one manager gets fired, another takes his place. Such was the case when the Angels fired Buck Rodgers in mid-May of 1994. The Angels hired their former pitching coach, Marcel Lachemann, to join the team as his replacement. Among the new manager's moves was to bring a longtime company man to the major leagues.

Joe Maddon was serving the Angels in a dual role at the time, working as the director of player development as well as the minor league field coordinator. Since Lachemann and Maddon had a relationship, Lachemann knew Maddon had over-the-top organizational skills and that he brought a different mindset to the table. Lachemann figured he'd be the perfect addition to his staff, so he called to tell Maddon he wanted him to be his bullpen coach. After receiving the call, an emotional Maddon called his mother to deliver the news: her 40-year-old son had made it to The Show. Then they cried into their respective phones at opposite ends of the country.

"It was a very emotional day for me," Maddon told the *Orange County Register*. "Because it was something I was always geared toward, getting to the major leagues as a coach.

"It's something we all strive to do. And, after 13 years in the minor leagues, I was [in the major leagues]. But, by the same token, it was amazing, because for as long as it was, it seemed like no time had passed when it finally happened. It seemed like you started yesterday."

Maddon had served in the Angels' organization as a player, manager, instructor, coach, scout, and supervisor, affording him ample opportunity to touch the lives of many players on their journey to the major leagues. Once he got the job, shortstop Gary DiSarcina gushed about him being one of the more positive people he'd been around in baseball.

Rex Hudler signed with the Angels as a free agent in March of 1994. At that time, the veteran utility man had played for renowned managers such as Whitey Herzog, Yogi Berra, Billy Martin, Earl Weaver, and Joe Torre. From that collection, he'd gathered a lot of different approaches to the game, and he'd witnessed a lot of baseball wisdom. But when Maddon came aboard, he allowed that he'd never quite experienced anybody like him during his career, which began in 1978.

"He brought a freshness, an enthusiasm that was welcomed by me, and maybe not some of the other guys, because they were thinking that Joe was a rah-rah, college-type coach," Hudler said. "I thought it was fresh. And I encouraged the veteran players that were on the team at the time to accept him. 'We need that from a coach, let's love on him, and bring him in.' That's positive. That's good. That's what you wanted. That didn't come from the manager, either. That came from a coach who had energy, had passion, had ideas."

Hudler complimented Lachemann for letting Maddon "do his thing."

"Marcel Lachemann recognized Joe's talent and brought him in," Hudler said.

Hudler respected the way Maddon "implemented his own style—no matter how it got laughed at by others.... When I talk to Joe now—we've been friends ever since then—and he says that he appreciates me telling the other guys to accept him back then," Hudler said. "I was in his corner the whole way. That formed a great relationship. I'm proud of what he's accomplished and done over the years. But I'm not a bit surprised."

Maddon's presence began to make an impact.

Later that summer, Chad Curtis told ESPN that the team's hitting coach, Rod Carew, did not communicate well. In fact, the Angels center fielder said Carew had not talked to him for three months. Carew had labeled Curtis as uncoachable, characterizing him as the personification of the modern player who didn't listen. Curtis noted that it wasn't right for Carew to label him as uncoachable when Carew never talked to him.

"If someone says, 'You did that wrong; do it this way,' I ask why," Curtis told the *Long Beach Press Telegram*. "Some people look at me like they're thinking, *Who do you think you are, questioning me?* But I'm just trying to learn.

"Some people take it the wrong way. Two people who didn't are [outfield instructor] Sam Suplizio and Joe Maddon. When Joe would tell me something, he would always tell me why. I think Rod and Buck Rodgers misinterpreted it. When Buck would tell me something and I'd ask why, he'd grit his teeth, like he's thinking, *Why is this guy questioning me?*"

Maddon had evolved in the old-school environment. From surviving in that element, he knew how to avoid ruffling feathers with those in the game who clung to prehistoric ideas, many based on "the book" of baseball dos and don'ts. He'd never played in the major leagues and some of the coaches and managers he dealt with had. And the players he coached were major leaguers. Still, he had enough presence of mind and confidence to stay the course and be himself. Why act old school when he had progressive ideas? Still, one of Maddon's constant battles was bringing computer technology into the game, and all the quality information that came with it. He explained the landscape to the *Long Beach Press-Telegram*.

"I think every manager would do it," Maddon said. "Take the word 'computer' out of it, go to any manager, and tell him he can have five years' worth of information on Don Mattingly—the location of every pitch he hit and every pitch that got him out, where he hit every ball, everything. Who wouldn't want that? But put the word 'computer' in there, and that's where the problem is. It's just information."

Individual battles aside, Maddon enjoyed being in the major leagues, noting that everything went by in a blur and that he was constantly in motion. He thought he'd been busy in the minor leagues, but he felt busier and more useful at the major league level. Defining the work that needed to be done felt more logical where daily preparation was concerned, and how to relate to veteran major league players who had enjoyed success. Life in the major leagues added up to a lot more for Maddon to do than what he was doing in the minor leagues.

Maddon arrived at spring training the following season as the Angels' first base coach, and he again brought fresh ideas to the game.

"You have to respect old school in our game," Hudler said. "Back then they wrote on the chalkboard at spring training:

stretch at 8:00, infield at 9:15, long-toss, then BP at 11:00, and wind sprints. And that was all written on the chalkboard. That was every day. Guys would check out. Some of them didn't even read the thing. Then Joe started putting out computer sheets."

Hudler credited Maddon for doing something "nobody else did."

"And I'd played a lot of baseball by the time I got to the Angels," Hudler said.

Maddon timed Angels hitters running to first base after they made contact. After gathering his data, he posted the top three times recorded on the board.

"I was like, 'You know what, this is fresh. I like this, it's brand new. It's stuff that we need to embrace,'" Hudler said. "We started competing with each other, going 90 feet. I know Joe's always respected 90 feet. And he talked about that. That helped in internal competition. That told me I wanted one of the top times, so I'm going to bust it out of the box."

Hudler recalled that Maddon also began to put a "Quote of the Day" on the bulletin board, and he used his computer to crunch numbers that he displayed on the board as well.

"Ten guys would be standing there at the board trying to read his quote of the day, and the computer stuff," Hudler said. "Guys are like, *What is this?* And that was the computer. He was changing things. And that's when it evolved for me and a lot of guys. Joe had his fingerprints all over that."

Hudler thought the quote of the day was "corny" and he and his teammates enjoyed some laughs "a lot of times."

"But it would permeate our brains, and we'd bring it up as a team during stretch," Hudler said. "Laughing with each other, so it built chemistry and camaraderie. It was special and I really appreciated him for that. He was an eclectic guy. He also has a way of being able to massage a player's mentality. As a player, you forget about the pressure. That's big in baseball. Joe was a lot like your father, a mentor, and a friend."

The Angels showed improvement in 1995, after going 47–68 in the strike-shortened 1994 season, but the season ended in heartbreak.

The Angels were the toast of the American League for the way they played in the first 5½ months of the season. They appeared on cruise control to win the American League West, holding a 10½-game lead over the Texas Rangers and an 11½-game lead over the Seattle Mariners on August 16. Then the team fell into a funk. The first big blow came when they lost nine in a row from August 25 to September 3. At the end of that skid, they still led the Mariners by six games and the Rangers by 7½. Then they suffered another nine-game losing streak from September 13 to 23, which knocked them out of first place. Somehow, they managed to rise from the dead to win their final five games to finish in a tie with the Mariners and force a one-game playoff. Playing in Seattle, the "Big Unit"—Randy Johnson, twirled a three-hitter and the Mariners took a 9–1 win to win the division.

"Man, that was brutal," Maddon said. "All season long, we were killing teams, really beating them up. Then everything just fell apart. Man, going through that was awful."

Maddon described feeling a weight in the clubhouse.

"We just needed one or two guys to go out there and lift that weight," Maddon said. "It didn't happen. Walking into that clubhouse, it just felt heavy. A lot of gloom and doom."

Maddon became the Angels' bench coach in 1996, in what turned out to be a turbulent season.

Throughout, he continued to perform any duty needed to help the team.

"Rod Carew was my hitting coach, and the best hitting coach I ever had in my 21-year career," Hudler said. "Mickey Vernon was right there with him. But Joe Maddon, he helped me, too. He liked my toe-tap. That was the toe-tap where you start out and then you tap your toe, and it loads your weight, and then you fire your hips and your hands come through. He was the one who would really compliment me on my hitting style."

Hudler had his best major league season in 1996 when he hit .311 with 16 home runs and 40 RBIs.

"I had one good year in 21 years, and 1996 was the year," Hudler said. "Joe, Rod Carew, and Chili Davis—who was a teammate of mine at the time—all had a big part in that."

Hudler's success in 1996 paved the way for him to sign a two-year, $2.3 million contract with the Phillies.

In early August of 1996, Lachemann resigned as the Angels manager, conceding that he could no longer motivate his team. John McNamara, who had managed the team from 1983 to 1984, was hired to manage the team for the remainder of the season.

Shortly thereafter, McNamara began to experience trouble getting around due to a calf muscle that doctors diagnosed as a strain. At first, he ran games from the office, using a walkie-talkie to communicate with Maddon. When McNamara's swollen leg continued to bother him, the diagnosis changed. The 64-year-old interim manager had a blood clot in his right calf and was admitted into New York's Presbyterian Columbia Medical Center.

Maddon got promoted to interim manager. He began his tenure on August 21 at Yankee Stadium. The Angels won 7–1 that night, and Maddon filled up the reporters' notebooks—after a shot of Jack Daniels, served up by Peter Bavasi, the brother of Angels general manager Billy Bavasi. Though unaccustomed at meeting with the media, he came through, acknowledging that Yankee Stadium was "a little different."

"It's like going to the Vatican," Maddon told reporters.

Days later, a reporter asked Maddon—who was the Angels' third manager of the season at that point—what they should call him. Maddon quipped, "Interim squared is fine."

Dealing with the media would become one of Maddon's strongest suits.

After the Angels moved to 3–0 under their second interim manager, they took a 5–4 loss to the Orioles in Baltimore. In the second inning of that loss, Maddon argued a check swing with third-base umpire Mike Reilly, and got ejected—his first in the major leagues. Maddon continued to call the shots from the clubhouse, enlisting a clubhouse boy to deliver messages to the Angels' bench.

"Since I was there in 1996, I can claim that Joe Maddon was one of my managers so I can claim him for the tremendous list of managers I played for," Hudler said. "I'm proud of that. When Marcel quit, Johnny McNamara came on to help. Johnny was a little old and broken down at the time. I played for Joe for some of those interim games. I'm proud of that.... There's not a player in the history of the game who played for all of the managers I did, so I'm really grateful for that."

Maddon began to receive endorsements to become the Angels' full-time manager less than a week into his interim assignment, and his 4–1 start.

Veteran Chili Davis asked the *Orange County Register*, "Why not give him a shot? You look at how we're playing right now, and that says a lot about him.... Everyone's laid back now and feeling really confident. Joe has a lot to do with that. And his moves are sensible. I think he deserves a shot at it."

Tim Salmon told *The* (Riverside, California) *Press-Enterprise*: "Should he be a managerial candidate? I don't know if I'm in a position to say that about anybody, but I will say that he's got some very good coaching tools. He sees things about the game that have impressed me."

Maddon stressed in the same article that he wasn't auditioning to become a manager. "I'm just doing a job because John McNamara's not here."

Later he told the *Orange County Register*: "I've never campaigned for any job I've received. I'm not going to do it here."

McNamara returned to the team on September 13 and managed for the remainder of the season. Maddon finished 8–14, concluding his tenure with an 11–2 loss at Cleveland. McNamara complimented the job Maddon did.

"Joe did an excellent job under some adverse circumstances," McNamara told the *Orange County Register* upon his return.

"Stepping in the middle of something like that is not an easy thing to do."

Maddon managed to keep his sense of humor throughout, even after he no longer managed the team. When the Angels hazed their rookies by stealing their clothes at a late-season game, replacing them with costumes and women's clothes, Maddon observed infielder George Arias in a racy orange dress and noted, "If George was my daughter, I wouldn't let him out of the house."

After the season concluded, Maddon's name could be found on the list of candidates being considered by the Angels to become the team's next manager.

Maddon might have been viewed by some as the Angels' answer for filling their managerial post for 1997, others believed they needed a disciplinarian. Hudler didn't think Maddon was ready to manage at the time.

"He was a good coach, but he was just finding his way as a coach," Hudler said.

In addition to Maddon, the list of candidates included Jim Leyland, Ken Macha, Tim Johnson, Davey Lopes, Rick Down, Sparky Anderson, Mike Cubbage, Jerry Narron, Jimy Williams, and Terry Collins.

The Angels first offered the job to Leyland. The longtime manager of the Pittsburgh Pirates turned them down, noting the job wasn't a good fit. (Leyland then accepted an offer from the Florida Marlins, who won the World Series in seven games over the Indians the next fall.) After Leyland passed on the job, Collins became the choice.

Collins' resume resembled Maddon's. He'd spent 10 seasons as a minor league player, never making it to the majors, and he'd set his sights on managing in 1981. That pursuit culminated in him getting his first managerial job in 1994 with the Houston Astros. After three winning seasons, he was fired following the 1996 campaign.

Maddon had a contract with the Angels through the 1997 season, but Collins had the freedom to keep or hire the coaches he wanted on his staff. After interviewing Maddon, Collins knew he wanted him to be his bench coach.

Maddon had the freedom under Collins to present his ideas.

"[I] had a great time with [Collins]," Maddon told the *Philadelphia Inquirer.* "We had a really good relationship on the bench, really good.... He always gave me a lot of latitude, permitted me to work. The thing about being a bench coach for him that I was always impressed with was, if I had a bunch of information, I would just stand there and I would read it to him, I'd talk to him about it before the game, and he would never forget anything."

Among the ideas Maddon presented to Collins that he approved was a shift against Ken Griffey Jr. Maddon based his suggestion on the charts he kept that revealed the Seattle slugger's tendencies.

Gary DiSarcina played shortstop for the Angels. He'd always fondly remembered Maddon as the roving hitting instructor full of positive vibes, and the guy who cared about him as a person. But he began to see him in a different light during the 1997 season. DiSarcina had gone on an Angels caravan accompanied by Maddon and others to speak at a rotary luncheon and miscellaneous different stops. When he listened to Maddon speak, he was blown away.

"He had it all, telling his story," DiSarcina said. "He explained how he did things. He had good stories, he was funny. He had it all. At that point, I began to think, *This guy would be a great manager.*"

Maddon continued to wear a lot of hats as the Angels bench coach. To Troy Percival, Maddon was a confidant.

"Even when I got to the big leagues, I had Joe Maddon," Percival said. "And when I was struggling, he was one of my go-to guys. He knew how to make me feel positive. Joe had been there since Day 1.

"Joe has always been the guy, whether he morphed or changed, he's always been the guy who thought on multiple layers, from the day he was our bench coach all the way to the day when he was the minor league director. He was always the same guy. He thinks on so many different levels."

Maddon remained a hands-on coach, too, which paid off for catchers Matt Walbeck and Phil Nevin.

In the spring of 1998, regular Angels catcher Todd Greene was on the disabled list following shoulder surgery, meaning the Angels needed production from Walbeck and Nevin.

Walbeck had always played catcher. Nevin had a different story.

The Houston Astros had selected the standout third baseman from Cal-State Fullerton with the first overall pick of the 1992 June draft. Nevin struggled offensively, prompting the Astros to trade him to the Detroit Tigers in 1995. The Tigers then traded him to the Angels, along with Walbeck after 1997.

Nevin attempted to re-invent himself during the 1996 season when he went down to the minor leagues to learn how to become a catcher. He caught 62 games for Double-A Jacksonville, then he caught four for the Tigers. He caught just one game for the Tigers in 1997.

Maddon took Walbeck and Nevin under his wing in the spring of 1998. Looking at the work ethic shared by each catcher, Maddon knew they were coachable. He considered all the drill work being done at other positions and asked the question: Why not implement catching drills?

He began to work both on blocking balls in the dirt, and having a quick release. Progress came quickly. Nevin threw out nine of 10 runners that spring, and Walbeck began the season by throwing out six of 10 runners. And the Angels felt better about their catching situation.

Walbeck gave all the credit to Maddon.

"The practice and repetition takes all the doubt out of my mind," Walbeck told the *Orange County Register*. "He just got me to trust my quickness, to basically not try to rush it."

Nevin started 62 games at catcher during the 1998 season.

When the Angels traded Nevin to the San Diego Padres in March of 1999, he spoke of Maddon.

"The toughest guy to say good-bye to was Joe Maddon," Nevin told the *Orange County Register*. "All the work we've done. Catching got me a job, catching will keep me a job. Really, he's the one who taught me everything."

Typical of Maddon, he praised Nevin in the same article.

"It's great working with somebody with a lot of skill, and he truly has improved," Maddon said. "…I really believe if he gets a chance to play on a regular basis, he will do well. The skill is there."

Nevin became an All-Star catcher in 2001, a season that saw his offense resemble his old Cal-State Fullerton days with a .306 average, 41 home runs, and 126 RBIs for the Padres.

In early June of 1998, the Angels and the Royals got into two bench-clearing brawls during the Angels' 7–5 win in Kansas City. The first got started when Jim Pittsley hit Nevin with a pitch and Nevin charged. Retaliation came when Angels hurler Mike Holtz hit Jose Offerman. In the aftermath of the incidents, American League president Gene Budig issued the following statement:

"The events of June 2, 1998, warrant severe disciplinary action on the part of the American League. Such altercations undercut the image of the game and the many efforts to regain public favor."

Budig went on to punish 11 members of the two teams.

Maddon came away with a fine. Collins received an eight-game suspension, which led to Maddon serving a stint as the interim manager. During that stint, the Angels won six of eight games.

Highly touted prospects such as DiSarcina and outfielders Garret Anderson, Tim Salmon, Jim Edmonds, and Darin Erstad were all in place with the major league club by 1998. And the Angels had respectable second-place finishes in the American League West Division in 1997 and 1998, posting records of 84–78 and 85–77, respectively. Collins appeared to be getting the job done. A little more help on the field appeared to be all that was needed.

Mo Vaughn appeared to be the answer. He'd hit .337 with 40 home runs and 115 RBIs in 1998, which proved to be perfect timing since he became a free agent after the season.

Vaughn took American League Most Valuable Player honors in 1995, and he'd been an All-Star in 1995, 1996, and 1998. Most viewed the former Seton Hall standout as the leader of the Red Sox. How could the Angels not bite on a free agent so attractive? They couldn't help themselves, and did bite, signing Vaughn to a six-year, $80 million deal that ranked as the highest contract in the majors at that time. Expectations and enthusiasm were high entering the 1999 season.

Unfortunately for Collins and the Angels, most everything that could go wrong did, including injuries and a less-than-harmonious clubhouse.

Vaughn, DiSarcina, Edmonds, and Salmon, along with pitchers Ken Hill, Jason Dickson, Tim Belcher, Pep Harris, Jack McDowell, and Mike James, all missed extended periods of time due to injuries.

The Angels still appeared to be on the right track at the All-Star break before winning just 10 of their next 47 games to land them in last place in the American League East.

Randy Velarde got traded to Oakland after the second baseman took shots at Collins. More disharmony in the clubhouse followed, capped by an incident that prompted Percival to speak out after a brawl in Cleveland brought less than total participation from his Angels teammates.

Cleveland's Richie Sexson had ignited the fire when he got a little too showy in celebrating a three-run homer against

Percival. The blast capped a 10-run rally for the Indians. Percival retaliated by drilling the next batter, David Justice.

Vaughn had been one of the players not going onto the field. In Vaughn's defense, he noted that he'd been in the clubhouse and hadn't been able to make it out onto the field in time. Upon hearing Percival's complaint, Vaughn told the media that nobody on the Angels' staff had retaliated on his behalf. He also directed a shot in Percival's direction when he noted that Percival should not have hit Justice. He added, "Take a beating like a man and get the next out."

Clearly, things weren't working, which prompted a meeting between Collins and general manager Bill Bavasi. At the meeting, they concluded Collins should resign. And he did, less than three months after he'd signed his extension.

With tears in his eyes, Collins resigned, telling a media gathering, "The bottom line is, the team's got to perform. When you don't perform, the manager's accountable. I had a feeling today that this is the time. I tried everything I knew, from patting them on the back to try to motivate them to kicking them in the butt."

The Angels then turned over the managerial duties to Maddon.

"The best way to describe it is to say I'm glad to have this opportunity, but the way it happened subtracts from any joy I feel," said Maddon at a press conference. "Terry and I had a great working relationship. I respect Terry. He taught me a lot."

He added: "I can do the job. Last time, I felt good but I realized I was not quite ready."

Maddon's first game at the helm came on September 3, 1999, against the Yankees in Anaheim. Maddon was 45 at the time. The Angels took an 8–2 win at Edison Field that night and finished out the season with a 19–10 run under Maddon.

The Angels' September 11 game against the Twins at Minnesota's Metrodome proved to be particularly memorable.

Eric Milton started an unusual morning game for the Twins that day, and the rookie left-hander put himself in the record books by no-hitting the Angels in a 7–0 Twins win. From the Angels' side, the interesting part came in the fact that Maddon started a lineup of reserves—and rookie Troy Glaus, for the unusual game that started at 11:06 in the morning. The starting time derived from the fact a college football game between Minnesota and Louisiana-Monroe was scheduled to take place at the Metrodome and stadium workers needed time to get the park prepared.

Four of the players in the Angels' lineup had been called up in September, and another got his call up in August. Rookie Jerry DaVanon, who was making his first major league start and did not have a major league hit, swung and missed at a 94-mph Milton fastball to end the game.

The criticism of Maddon came in the fact that he didn't bring any of his veteran players off the bench to try and spoil Milton's gem.

"Some of us were telling Joe by about the sixth inning that we wanted to get in there," DiSarcina said. "But Joe stuck to his guns. He'd told us he we were going to have the day off. He didn't go back on what he told us. That showed me something. The guy sticks to his word."

Maddon explained that had no regrets about his decision, and had he been put in that same situation again, he would not have done anything differently. He had decided to go with the lineup he started for the entire game. Once Milton's no-hitter began to appear like a possibility, he didn't have second thoughts since the Angels were already down seven runs. Maddon further noted that the situation presented an opportunity to build team unity among the players who weren't playing. He concluded that his idea wasn't wrong, it simply had not worked.

Prior to the start of the 1999 season, Maddon had bought his father a satellite dish so he could watch Angels games on television. Given the time difference, staying up could be difficult for Joe Sr., but not quite as hard once Joe took over as the team's interim manager.

At the very least, he felt good about what he'd accomplished in the aftermath of Collins leaving.

"There was not a real good clubhouse at that time," Maddon told the *Worcester Telegram & Gazette* (Massachusetts). "There were a lot of disenchanted players. It was a hostile environment. But I thought we brought the clubhouse back together, got the players to play for pride, got them to believe in themselves."

Clearly, Maddon had served his apprenticeship. He'd paid his dues. But would that be enough to entice the Angels to finally hire him as their full-time manager?

7

Scioscia Takes Over

THE ANGELS' EXTENSIVE SEARCH FOR A NEW MANAGER GOT underway once the 1999 season concluded. Maddon's name could be found among the usual list of candidates, including Phil Garner, Kevin Kennedy, Willie Randolph, Davey Lopes, Don Baylor, and Chris Chambliss.

Before the search got too far along, the Angels brought in a new general manager. Bill Stoneman took over for Bill Bavasi, who had resigned three days before the final games of the 1999 season.

Maddon's interview with Stoneman took place at the general managers' meetings in Dana Point, California. At those same meetings, Stoneman interviewed Mike Scioscia.

Scioscia had been born and bred a Los Angeles Dodger. He played 1,441 games wearing Dodger blue from 1980 to 1992.

A bulldog of a catcher during his playing days, Scioscia had a reputation for being a pillar of granite when blocking the plate. He'd been a big part of the Dodgers' 1981 and 1988 World Series champion teams. Of note, he hit a dramatic, ninth-inning, game-tying home run off the New York Mets' Dwight Gooden in Game 4 of the 1988 National League Championship Series. The Dodgers went on to win that game in extra innings, making Scioscia's round-tripper a pivotal moment to help the Dodgers capture that series.

Famed Dodgers manager Tommy Lasorda had this to say about Scioscia becoming his starting catcher: "When I made Mike the No. 1 catcher, the writers came to me and said, '[Competing catcher] Steve Yeager said you made Scioscia the No. 1 catcher because he's Italian.' I said, 'That's a lie. I made him the No. 1 catcher because I'm Italian.'"

After he retired, Scioscia went on to serve as the Dodgers' minor league catching coordinator, and the bench coach, prior to a stint managing the Pacific Coast League's Albuquerque Dukes during the 1999 season. He resigned from his position managing the Dukes after the season, telling the Dodgers he wanted to explore opportunities in other organizations.

Then Scioscia became the Angels' new manager.

Upon the announcement of Scioscia's hiring, the Angels' new manager announced his coaching staff. Only Maddon was retained from the previous year's staff.

Rod Carew, who had won seven batting titles en route to the Hall of Fame, highlighted the list of coaches that got replaced. Also on that list were third-base coach Larry Bowa, pitching coach Dick Pole, and first-base coach George Hendrick.

Mickey Hatcher took over as the team's hitting coach. Bud Black became the pitching coach, Alfredo Griffin the first-base coach, and Ron Roenicke the third-base coach. Other than Maddon and Black, the new selections had Dodger ties.

Maddon still aspired to become a major league manager, but allowed that it wasn't going to happen with the Angels.

"Mike's here and I think it's great," Maddon told the *Orange County Register*. "I think he's perfect for this group. I'm happy to be part of it. But if the right situation were to come along, I'll stay ready."

Though the team had finished the 1999 season at 70–92 to finish fourth in the American League West, they had a lot of young talent on the roster, including Salmon, Glaus, Erstad, and Anderson. Maddon had influenced many of them along the way, like Glaus.

"He's one of my favorite guys I've ever met in the game," Glaus told the *Allentown Morning Call.* "He really helped me with his ability to stay even-keeled all the time. I was a young player when I first met him. Maybe it was the same message that three or four other people had said, but the way he put it, I always understood it. And he was always prepared, there's no doubt about that. There wasn't a bit of information he hadn't gone over at least once, and probably twice."

When the team traveled to Baltimore, Maddon's father and mother were there, making the trip from Hazleton with steak and cheese hoagies and cold pizza, so they could celebrate Father's Day together.

Maddon had already experienced the thrill of having his parents see him wearing a major league uniform in Yankee Stadium, but he relished re-living that experience in other ballparks. This stop seemed to resonate more with Maddon since his father had reached 80, had congestive heart failure, had experienced a mild heart attack in the spring, and had recently been diagnosed with prostate cancer.

"I love being able to provide this," Maddon told *The Orange County Register.* "Where he can come to a major league park, hang out in the lobby of the hotel and meet the guys. He loves baseball."

Scioscia's first season saw an Angels team fueled by offense go 82–80, and remain in the playoff chase until late in the season.

Erstad led the way with 240 hits, a .355 average, 25 home runs, 100 RBIs, 121 runs scored, and 28 stolen bases. Glaus won the American League home run race with 47, setting an Angels record. Anderson, Vaughn, and Salmon chipped in with 35, 36, and 34 home runs, respectively.

The offense set a club record with 236 home runs. Unfortunately for the Angels, their pitching did not match the excellence of the offense. None of the team's starters managed to pitch even 170 innings, and reliever Shigetoshi Hasegawa's 10 wins, along with his 3.57 ERA, led the team.

On the bright side, the culture inside the clubhouse began to change. Negative gave way to positive, making the future of the team look bright.

Maddon and Scioscia began to forge what became a solid relationship in 2000. Scioscia liked what Maddon brought to the table.

"I don't know if 'eccentric' is the right word for Joe," Scioscia said. "He's an extremely intelligent person; he's just really bright. He has a fine spirit that is really beautiful to be around. It's beautiful to talk baseball with him, life with him. He's got a really unique perspective on things."

Scioscia noted that Maddon had "an incredible classic foundation for baseball fundamentals, combined with the idea that maybe there's a better mousetrap out there—whether it's developing a player or instilling in a player coming up in the minor leagues qualities that are going to help you win in the big leagues."

Scioscia also loved the daily information Maddon provided him, such as spray charts, which showed the direction in which opposing hitters typically hit the ball, and other valuable tidbits throughout the game that helped Scioscia make informed decisions.

While Maddon embraced the analytics of the game way in advance of analytics driving the game as they later would, he had perspective about their use.

"You're talking about people," Maddon told the *Worcester Telegram & Gazette* (Massachusetts). "They count more than things in a box [computer]. [With statistics], you're just trying to give the players an edge. But it depends on how much each player can handle."

While Scioscia benefitted from having Maddon on his staff, Maddon learned a lot from Scioscia, too. He embraced his technique for blocking the plate, which varied from the traditional method used by most catchers at the time—before there were rules about tagging runners and blocking the plate.

In deference to holding the baseball in his bare hand inside the catcher's mitt to make the tag, Scioscia tagged runners with the ball in his glove, sans his throwing hand. He also went against the grain by going to both knees while waiting for a throw to home, rather than one or standing, and he'd position himself turned slightly sideways. That way, if he got trucked by the baserunner, he might get knocked backwards, but there was less of a chance to injure his legs.

"With Sciosh, it's about consistency," Maddon told the *Worcester Telegram & Gazette*. "It's about being the same every day. It's about not backing down from the promise about attacking that problem, not allowing things to fester. It's about humor. It's about keeping the guys up every day. It's about communication. It's about doing everything with a passion and at the same time keeping things in their proper perspective."

Rex Hudler returned to the Angels to do the color for the TV broadcasts. Plunked down among Maddon and Scioscia, Hudler noted that he saw a different Maddon.

"He had evolved," Hudler said. "As the bench coach, he had evolved into someone who could be a major league manager. Scioscia empowered him to let him do his thing, and he did his thing. He was a great bench coach. He was made for that role. To prepare, to get the computer reads, do all that stuff to prepare his manager for that day's work. And then he evolved into a manager and that's just a natural step for a guy like him who is as good as he is."

After Scioscia's inaugural season, the Angels took a backward step in 2001, slipping to 75–87 and another third-place finish in the American League West.

The pitching showed improvement, as the starting rotation became a strength. Ramon Ortiz won 13 games, while Jarrod Washburn and Scott Schoeneweis each won 10. Meanwhile, the offense that had been so strong the previous year, underachieved.

The high point of the season coincided with Maddon's fun side on August 19, at the end of a three-game series at Cleveland's Jacobs Field. When players checked the lineup

Maddon had posted in the visiting lineup for the Sunday afternoon game, they found each player listed by a nickname.

The names were clever, issued in the spirit of Bluto from *Animal House* when tagging the Delta pledges. Among those were the following: Jorge Fabregas was "Gasolina." Scott Spiezio was "Spaz." Catcher Bengie Molina was "El Cerebro" because he was the brains behind the plate. Jeff Da Vanon: "Yogurt," Adam Kennedy: "A.F.K.," and there was Shawn Wooten, who packed 225 pounds on his 5'10" frame. He was "Flaco" (Spanish translation: *skinny*).

Dubbed accordingly, El Cerebro, A.F.K., and company went out and took a 4–1 win over the Indians with 42,510 watching.

Washburn picked up the win that day to give the Angels a series win, moving the team to eight games over .500 and to within six games of the A's for the American League Wild Card spot.

The next day, Angels management signed Scioscia to a contract extension through the 2005 season.

Then the bottom fell out.

The Angels went 9–29 after August 19, including 19 losses in their final 21 games.

Amid the perplexing offensive problems was Mo Vaughn's absence following elbow surgery, causing him to miss the whole season. Salmon hit just .227 with 17 home runs and 49 RBIs. Erstad hit just .258, which was a far cry from his previous season. Glaus did manage to again hit at least 40 home runs and drive in 100, but even he suffered through prolonged slumps.

Meanwhile the Seattle Mariners, under manager Lou Piniella, tied a major league record with 116 wins to run away with the American League West division and the Oakland A's rode a hot second half to get into the playoffs as the Wild Card.

That left the Angels in third place, 41 games out of first.

If there was a bright side, it came wrapped in the character of the team. They never quit, even after their season went south. Scioscia went so far as to thank his players for their effort following the season. The team also had chemistry and a foundation that they could build upon for the 2002 season.

8

A Sad Time,
Then Euphoria

THE 2002 ANGELS ENTERED THE SEASON WITH A 500-POUND gorilla on their back. How does a team go about bridging the gap after finishing 41 games out of first place the previous season?

For starters, the Angels traded Mo Vaughn to the New York Mets for right-hander Kevin Appier.

A precursor for Vaughn's Angels career had come when he fell down the dugout steps on the first play of his first game as an Angel. He came away from the freak accident with a sprained ankle.

When healthy, Vaughn had hit well for the Angels, with 30 home run, 100 RBI seasons in 1999 and 2000. But he had missed all of 2001, and the more the Angels thought about it, the more they liked the idea of having Scott Spiezio at first and using Vaughn to acquire a starting pitcher.

Troy Percival chirped about Vaughn after the trade, noting, "We may miss Mo's bat, but we won't miss his leadership. Darin Erstad is our leader."

Vaughn fired back by saying that Percival and the Angels hadn't done anything in the history of their franchise, adding, "They ain't got no flags hanging at friggin' Edison Field, so the hell with them."

Those words would prove to be memorable. But the way the season began, some probably thought Vaughn had made some valid points.

Maddon's world got turned upside down in mid-April when he got the news that his father had died. Numb and full of emotions all at once, and knowing that he'd never again see the man he loved and respected so, Maddon left the team and headed to Pennsylvania for the funeral.

While away, Maddon managed to watch the Angels on the satellite dish he'd bought for his father, and what he saw wasn't good.

"My impression watching the guys on TV was that they looked a little down," Maddon told the *Orange County Register*.

The Angels were following up their horrendous 2001 finish with the worst start in franchise history by going 6–14.

Morale quickly picked up with the eight-game winning streak that followed. That streak launched a stretch that saw the Angels go 21–3, which completely changed the complexion of the team. Rather than boppers, the Angels became scrappers and masters of playing the game the right way. Along the way, they learned how to win the close games.

Some of what began to happen could be credited to chemistry and a much-improved starting staff and the work of the bullpen. Another part of the equation could be credited to the approach sold at spring training by Mike Scioscia, Maddon, and hitting coach Mickey Hatcher. The had a goal of creating a team that wasn't static.

The 2001 Angels had been ineffective at producing productive outs. They struggled to move runners, and they were subpar at hitting with runners in scoring position.

Hoping to help sell what they wanted from their offense, Scioscia, Hatcher, and Maddon met with Erstad, Anderson, Salmon, and Glaus, bringing them into Scioscia's office and asking for their feedback. The three things they stressed that were going to be deemed most important to the team's success were runs scored, RBIs, and on-base percentage. They also tried to raise the awareness of what was important in certain situations and to create within each player an approach for facing those situations.

In truth, the elixir the Angels coaches were selling was old-school fundamentals that every player on the team had heard about since Little League.

"It's beyond anything I've ever been a part of," Erstad told the *Orange County Register* when asked about the offense. "I love it. It's a full team of guys doing little things day in and day out. That's fun. We're getting runs by giving guys up."

Erstad described the effect the team's situational hitting had on opponents.

"It's like slow death," Erstad said. "You get a run here, get another the next inning, then maybe another one. Then all of a sudden, one of the big boys hits one."

Maddon did his part by creating situational charts. Of the 22 categories on his charts, 16 addressed what a player did at the plate, and six were for base running. For example, one report detailed the hits or walks that took place on two-strike counts, or how many runners scored from third base with less than two outs.

Initially, Maddon posted the charts for everyone's viewing. After a while, he no longer had to do so. The players had so thoroughly embraced the concepts that they didn't need to be reminded.

Maddon also felt like the team received some other help.

"I like to think my dad has something to do with it," Maddon told the *Orange County Register*. "There may be a little heavenly assistance involved."

The Angels finished four games behind the Athletics in the American League West. But their 99–63 record earned them a Wild Card playoff berth and their first appearance in the playoffs since 1986.

The team's .341 on-base percentage ranked fourth in the American League, which showed improvement from the previous season when they finished 10th (.327). The Angels scored 851 runs, which ranked fourth, compared with 691 (12th) in 2001. The Angels hit .316 with runners in scoring position after hitting .263 in 2001. They hit .257 with two out and runners in scoring position, which improved from .220 in 2001. And they finished third with 811 RBIs after finishing 13th (662) in 2001. Most importantly, the Angels posted the largest run differential in the major leagues, outscoring their opponents by 207 runs.

Garrett Anderson had the team's best offensive season, hitting .306 with 29 home runs and 123 RBIs.

Jarrod Washburn led the staff with an 18–6 record. Ramon Ortiz went 15–9 and Appier went 14–12. Aaron Sele and John

Lackey kicked in with 17 wins. Percival led the bullpen with 40 saves. Brendan Donnelly, Schoeneweis, Ben Weber, and Al Levine filled the bridge innings between the starter and Percival.

A raucous Anaheim crowd could be counted on during home games at Edison Field. When the Angels fell behind, inspiration would come from the "Rally Monkey," the team's motivation mascot that became more familiar as the season progressed.

When the Angels clinched, Maddon could be counted among the most emotional in the clubhouse. He'd been in the organization forever. He had seen so many of the players who were celebrating when they were at the beginning of their careers. And he'd helped them along their way to become major leaguers.

"You try not to be overly emotional, but so many things go through your mind," Maddon told the *Los Angeles Daily News*. "Watching Garret [Anderson] walk up to the on-deck circle in the seventh inning, I flashed back to [Rookie League] Mesa [Arizona], when I knew he didn't want to be there because he was better than everybody else.

"I remember watching Salmon at Grand Canyon College and saw him as a freshman hit two home runs in a game."

Maddon also thought about his father.

In the Division Series, the Angels were heavy underdogs to the Yankees. When the Yankees won the first game 8–5, most figured the favorites wearing pinstripes would go ahead and finish the job. Instead, the Angels won the next three games to advance to the American League Championship Series against the Minnesota Twins.

Playing at the Humbert H. Humphrey Metrodome, the hometown Twins won the first game of the series 2–1. The Angels then reeled off four consecutive wins to earn a spot in the World Series against the San Francisco Giants, which made for an all-California Fall Classic.

Once again, the Angels entered as underdogs to the Giants, and slugger Barry Bonds.

Baseball's career home run leader had set the single-season home run record in 2001 with 73, and he'd followed that season with 46 in 2002, so he still reigned as the best hitter in the game.

Sticking to the script, the Angels dropped the first game of the World Series 4–3 at home. Then the offense got busy, scoring 21 runs on 32 hits to win the next two games, giving the Angels a two games to one lead in the best-of-seven series.

Lackey started Game 4 for the Angels and controlled Bonds by intentionally walking him three times. Still, the Giants found a way, taking a 4–3 win at Pacific Bell Park. The following night, the Giants pounded out 16 hits in a 16–4 win in San Francisco, edging the Giants to within one victory of claiming the franchise's first World Series championship since relocating from New York to San Francisco.

Bonds dominated the World Series with his bat, hitting .471 with four home runs and six RBIs. But that contribution wasn't enough to overcome what the Angels accomplished in Game 6.

With the Angels trailing three games to two, the stage was set for the Angels to make their mark with a memorable comeback.

The Giants led 5–0 in Game 6 and appeared on cruise control for a victory parade. No team in World Series history had ever erased a five-run lead in a potential elimination game.

The willful Angels would not fold.

Spiezio hit a three-run homer off Giants starter Russ Ortiz in the seventh inning. Erstad added a solo home run off Tim Worrell in the eighth. After Salmon and Anderson singled, Glaus' two-run double drove home the tying and winning runs to force a Game 7.

With 44,598 watching the deciding game of the World Series at Edison Field, Anderson's double in the third scored three, giving the Angels a 4–1 lead.

Francisco Rodriguez put the icing on an amazing run when he struck out three in the eighth inning. The Angels had called up the 20-year-old rookie in September and he finished the postseason by claiming wins—all in relief—in five of the Angels' 11 wins.

Percival took over in the ninth, and the veteran closer retired Kenny Lofton on a flyout to center field to end the game and earn the Angels their first World Series championship.

Maddon told *Sports Illustrated*: "These guys play the game the way Abner Doubleday wrote it up."

In the aftermath of the resulting celebration, Maddon celebrated further by purchasing a Mitsubishi Outlander, which he drove across the country to Hazleton.

Once he arrived at his hometown, Maddon went to the house of his sister, Carmine Parlatore. She had a bow ready for her brother. He positioned the bow on top of the Outlander then presented the car to his mother, who had never had a new car in her life.

While in Hazleton, he served as the guest of honor at a reception at Lobitz Hall to raise money for a scholarship named after his late father. He also visited a classroom of second graders at Height-Terrace Elementary Middle School. The students had written a book they titled, "Joe Maddon Dreamed Big League Dreams." Maddon read the book to the students.

The hometown boy had done good.

9

Angels
Swan Song

ANGELS PLAYERS HAD A SPECIAL CHEMISTRY, WHICH THEY put on display with their World Series championship. But the bond and cohesiveness between manager Mike Scioscia and his coaches was equally as strong.

"Beyond intelligence or baseball knowledge is this group's ability to coexist, to disagree in a manner where we still get along," Maddon told the *Inland Valley Daily Bulletin* (Ontario, California). "Nobody needs to have it be their idea. Any business, any organization that can work in that environment is going to be successful."

All of the coaches were rewarded with two-year contracts, which was unusual, though pitching coach Bud Black wanted just one year.

The Angels began the 2003 season a different team because of what they accomplished the previous season, creating an invaluable experience.

"We did win," Maddon told the *Orange County Register*. "Once you have that experience to draw on, everything changes.... The World Series experience, the All-Star experience for some of us—that stretches you. We have something to hold on to now that we didn't have before as an organization. Philosophically, or however you want to describe it, we know it works."

Unfortunately for the Angels, a lot of what could go wrong did go wrong in 2003. Sometimes the ball just doesn't bounce a team's way.

All teams must deal with injuries, but the 2003 Angels experienced injuries, and then some.

Troy Glaus suffered a torn rotator cuff and frayed labrum in his right shoulder to end his season. Darin Erstad went on the disabled list with a hamstring problem that lingered for the length of the season. Designated hitter Brad Fullmer suffered a season-ending knee injury, and shortstop David Eckstein went on the disabled list with an inflamed nerve in his lower back.

On August 10, the Angels took a 3–1 loss to the Indians in Cleveland, giving them their 63rd loss of the season, or the number of losses they suffered for the entire 2002 campaign.

A 5–20 stretch after the All-Star break destroyed any hopes of repeating, and they finished the season with a disappointing 77–85 record to finish third in the American League East.

The Florida Marlins beat the Yankees in the Series to become World Champions for the second time in franchise history. But what happened during the Yankees' march to the postseason ended up affecting Maddon, and raised his hopes that he might finally get a shot at managing in the major leagues.

Boston Red Sox manager Grady Little had led the team to 93 and 95 wins in his two seasons with the Red Sox.

In the Red Sox's 2003 Division Series against the Oakland A's, the Red Sox had managed a comeback, winning the final three games to advance to the American League Championship Series against the hated New York Yankees.

After the Yankees took a 3–2 lead, the series moved to New York. At this point, Little appeared secure in assuming he'd be the Red Sox manager again in 2004. The Red Sox managed to take a win in Game 6 to force a deciding Game 7 in New York, and they would have ace Pedro Martinez—though on short rest—on the mound, giving the Red Sox the look of a team with everything lining up for a date in the Fall Classic.

Martinez and the Red Sox had a 4–2 lead after seven innings, and most assumed that Martinez was finished pitching. The Red Sox then scored in the eighth on a solo home run by David Ortiz. With a three-run lead to protect, Little sent Martinez back to the mound to pitch the eighth.

Martinez found trouble right away. Still, Little trusted his ace more than he trusted his bullpen, so he left in Martinez. The Yankees took advantage of the tired Red Sox ace and tied the game in the eighth, which set up Aaron Boone's walk-off homer against knuckleballer Tim Wakefield in the 11th inning.

Boston's fold, coupled with the fact that general manager Theo Epstein and owner John Henry were both advocates of analytics for assessing players and matchups and Little wasn't, spelled the end for Little, who was not retained as manager of the team after his contract expired and the team chose to not pick up his option for 2004.

The resulting vacancy opened the door for Maddon to manage the Red Sox once they asked the Angels for permission to talk to him about the job. The interview came in November.

Dodgers third-base coach Glenn Hoffman and A's bench coach Terry Francona were interviewed by the Red Sox prior to Maddon having his day with the Red Sox brass.

Epstein and assistant general manager Josh Byrnes interviewed Maddon in Phoenix during Major League Baseball's general managers' meetings.

After his interview, Maddon spoke on a conference call and told reporters that he felt as though the interview had gone well and that he'd been impressed by the thoroughness of the interview. He also noted that the thought of managing the Red Sox "would intimidate anyone."

"Anyone who said it didn't I think would be a liar," Maddon said. "It's ominous. It's an intimidating job, a big job. It's at the top of the baseball world. It's a job you would have to grow in to, learn to feel the pulse."

Despite the demands of the job, Maddon also said he felt qualified for the job, and up to the challenge of being the Red Sox manager.

"Intriguing is a better word," he said. "There would be a magic sense of managing from that dugout and looking out toward the Green Monster. Fenway Park is absolutely the most unique ballpark in baseball."

Maddon didn't get the job.

In early December, the Red Sox announced they had hired Francona. Maddon admitted that he was disappointed that he didn't get the job, but, as he told the *Standard-Speaker* (Hazleton, Pennyslvania), not to the extent "of crying in my Cheerios."

Along with that statement, Maddon complimented Francona and the Red Sox in how they had conducted their search to find a new manager. He came away feeling that he would learn from the experience and that what he learned would eventually lead him to his first managerial post in the major leagues.

"It was reassuring to go through this experience knowing who I was and what I strongly believe in," Maddon said. "You don't have to stray from your thoughts and beliefs to appeal to people. It's about being you. This reaffirmed my belief in myself."

In 2004, the Angels finished with a 92–70 mark to win the American League West before getting swept in three games during their Division Series against the Red Sox. The Red Sox went on to win the World Series in 2004.

Following the 2004 season, Maddon continued to be a hot name to be considered for open managerial positions. But nothing came to fruition, so Maddon returned to the Angels for the 2005 season. That season, they finished at 95–67 and again won their division. This time they defeated the Yankees in five games, which sent them on to face the Chicago White Sox in the American League Championship Series.

On October 16, 2005, at Angel Stadium of Anaheim, White Sox right-hander Jose Contreras held the Angels to three hits in a 6–3 win in Game 5 of the American League Championship Series. Not only did the defeat end the Angels season, it also marked the final game of Maddon's tenure with the Angels.

On the other side of the United States, the Tampa Bay Devil Rays were looking to make change.

10

A Franchise in Need

ON MARCH 9, 1995, THE TAMPA BAY DEVIL RAYS AND ARIZONA Diamondbacks became the 13th and 14th expansion teams in major league history by a vote by the owners of 28–0. Both teams began play in 1998.

By the end of the 2005 season, the Devil Rays had put eight seasons in the books. In that span, they finished last in the American League East every season save for 2004, when they went 70–91 to finish fourth in the five-team division.

From the beginning, much had gone wrong for the franchise that played in St. Petersburg, Florida, at Tropicana Field, a much-maligned indoor facility with plenty of quirks. Notable among those were the catwalks that batted balls occasionally struck. Some were ruled home runs, others were ruled foul balls, and, most interesting of all, some were ruled in play.

The Devil Rays, with their losing ways and quirky park, became an easy mark for those looking for humor.

If the building itself weren't bad enough, some of the mistakes made by the team during those first eight seasons were hard to believe. Others simply backfired, like in the case of Matt White.

The 6'5" right-hander from Waynesboro Area High School in Pennsylvania appeared to be the real deal. He'd been *USA Today's* National High School Player of the Year in 1996. Every amateur scout in baseball knew about White's arm.

The Giants had selected White with the seventh overall pick of the 1996 June Draft, but they had failed to offer White a contract before 15 days after the draft had passed. High-profile agent Scott Boras served as White's advisor and discovered a little-known codicil in the draft rules that he interpreted as a way for White to become a free agent. The loophole Boras discovered came in Rule 4E, which said a team must offer their draft picks a contract within 15 days of the draft. Major League Baseball agreed with Boras' interpretation, and White became a free agent.

The Devil Rays aggressively pursued White, a pitcher many felt could be the anchor of a major league staff for many years, and eventually they signed him for a $10.2 million bonus.

White was a great kid, and pitched well in the Devil Rays' farm system before injuries derailed his journey. He never pitched in the major leagues.

When the expansion draft took place the winter before the Devil Rays' first season, the Devil Rays selected outfielder Bobby Abreu. Believing that they would depend on their pitching in their first season, general manager Chuck LaMar felt like they needed to put a quality defensive team on the field to back up that pitching. That prompted the Devil Rays to ship Abreu to the Philadelphia Phillies for shortstop Kevin Stocker.

Stocker played two non-descript seasons for the Devil Rays. He never again played in the major leagues after the 2000 season. Abreu became an All-Star, hitting .291 while playing 18 seasons in the major leagues, collecting 2,470 hits along the way.

The Devil Rays signed right-hander Juan Guzman to a two-year, $12.5 million contract in 2000. Guzman had a spotty injury history and that turned out to be the case with the Devil Rays as well. He notched five outs in his first start for the Rays, got lifted due to injury, and never pitched in the major leagues again.

Other failed contracts included the troika of Greg Vaughn, Wilson Alvarez, and Vinny Castilla, whom the team directed $82 million in multi-year contracts to, and each failed in spectacular fashion.

Hope for the franchise came prior to the 2003 season, when Tampa native Lou Piniella came home to manage his hometown team, signing a four-year, $13 million contract.

Piniella had won a World Series while playing for the New York Yankees. He'd managed a World Series champion with the Reds in 1990 and been at the helm of the Seattle Mariners when they won 116 games in 2001. He brought with him a .537 winning percentage (1,319–1,135) earned from his tenures while managing the Yankees, Reds, and Mariners. Five of his teams went to the postseason.

The Devil Rays had shown a seven-game improvement from 2003 to 2004 when the team finished fourth. But the positive momentum didn't carry over to 2005, and the Devil Rays again finished in the basement. By the end of the 2005 season, Piniella had reached his boiling point.

He negotiated an exit deal with Stuart Sternberg, whose group paid $65 million for 48 percent of the team in May 2004. Sternberg would become the team's principal owner after the 2005 season, taking control from managing general partner

Vince Naimoli, who had led the charge to win a major league franchise for the Tampa Bay area in 1995. Naimoli had run the team as managing general partner to that point.

Piniella allowed that he didn't foresee things ending the way they did.

"There's always disappointment," Piniella told reporters. "When I signed on here three years ago, I didn't think it would end this way, obviously. If I thought it would, I probably would have chosen a different approach. But what are you going to do? I've done the best I can."

Piniella's main problem was a desire to win right away rather than go through the exercise of the building process.

"You've got a new ownership group taking over and they need to bring in their own manager that they can grow with," Piniella told reporters when the news of his departure became official. "At the same time, it will give me time to go home and relax and fish and play some golf. I'm tired. I need some time off."

The franchise appeared to be in total disarray.

"Lou Piniella had bought out of his contract," said Marc Topkin, who has covered the Tampa Bay franchise for the *Tampa Bay Times* since the team's inception. "They'd had a couple of rough years, and they'd had what was supposed to be a fairy tale situation, bringing Lou Piniella home to manage the team. His hometown team, a guy who'd won everywhere he'd been. I think everybody had grandiose expectations, including Lou Piniella. And it didn't work.

"Lou felt like Vince Naimoli had made certain promises about how he would make the team better and spend more money. That didn't happen. And so they were definitely at a low point in terms of on the field, and I think just where they were headed."

After Sternberg took control, he got busy.

Cutting loose general manager Chuck LaMar was one of his first moves.

LaMar had been the team's first and only general manager. Under his leadership, the Devil Rays put together a 518–775 record, which equated to one of the worst ever eight-year stretches for an expansion team.

LaMar issued the fans an apology in the aftermath of his firing, telling reporters on a conference call, "I take full responsibility for this organization not winning during the eight major league seasons that I've been here. It's the general manager's responsibility, no matter what the circumstances are, to find a way to put a winning product on the field."

LaMar also noted that he felt the group that came in, from general manager to manager, would be inheriting a cupboard that wasn't exactly bare.

"I believe this organization has one of the finest young groups of players in baseball," LaMar said. "By the 2007 season, the young players we have will get better, the next group of players will be performing at the major league level and for the first time since 1999–2000, the organization will be in the financial situation to put a significant amount of money into the club."

LaMar referred to the approximately $10 million in deferred payments the Devil Rays still owed players and Piniella for the 2006 season. After that, the financial picture would be a little more palatable.

A week later, Sternberg held a press conference at the Renaissance Vinoy Resort in St. Petersburg. After introducing himself, Sternberg noted, "The time has come for dramatic change for this organization… and we are intent on bringing that change to bear."

He then unveiled plans to try and connect with fans, business leaders, and potential sponsors. Only 1,141,669 fans had passed through the turnstiles in 2005, which ranked last in the major leagues.

The Devil Rays' slogan for the 2006 season was introduced as well: Under Construction.

"You open up the walls, and you never know what you're going to find sometimes," Sternberg said. "The contractor says, 'Whoa, look what we just found.' We don't know, but we're going in there and take a hammer to things…. We're going to do that by giving people the picks and shovels and forks and spoons and whatever they need to go in and dig and tell us what needs to be done.

"We will prioritize what needs to be done. The list is going to be—I'm a 35 sleeve—and it's going to be longer than my arm. And we're going to get at it. Some things are going to happen in a matter of minutes, days, weeks, months."

Hiring a new manager became the first order of business for the management team that consisted of new team president Matt Silverman, new team general manager Andrew Friedman—who took the title of executive vice president of baseball operations—and longtime baseball man Gerry Hunsicker, who was hired to serve in an advisory capacity.

Piniella had been a hardline manager, so a lot of the sentiment in the clubhouse was in favor of having a more communicative manager.

"I think it should be somebody who's a little laid-back and less intense but firm at the same time," left fielder Carl Crawford told the *Tampa Bay Times*. "Someone who's patient and can work well with and relate and talk to young kids because that's what we're dealing with here.

"I'm not saying I don't like Lou Piniella's style but I just think a lot of people were more nervous when they played. I think a lot of the young players were playing not to make mistakes because they didn't want to get hollered at or fussed at instead of just going out and playing their way."

And so, the search began.

"We are seeking a man of character; someone who is an excellent communicator, who is open to new ideas, and who can develop and grow with our players," said Silverman in a statement released by the club. "Most importantly, he should be excited by the opportunity and challenge to create a winning tradition with the Rays."

The Devil Rays looked internally first.

Bench coach John McLaren, first-base coach Billy Hatcher, third-base coach Tom Foley, and Triple-A Durham manager Bill Evers made up the first round of interviews.

Then came the names of other candidates.

Alan Trammell, who had just been fired by the Tigers, was on the list, which grew to include Yankees bench coach Joe Girardi, former Athletics manager Ken Macha, former Mets and Rangers manager Bobby Valentine, Braves hitting coach

Terry Pendleton, Hall of Fame third baseman Mike Schmidt, and Joe Maddon.

The job "is something I really want," said Maddon, who believed he would be a good fit for the job given the skills he had, which he felt were in line with what the Devil Rays wanted from their next manager. Managing a young, developing team appealed to him, as did working with Sternberg and the club's management team. Prior to his first interview, the Devil Rays sent him a 47-page email touting Sternberg's philosophies for turning around the Devil Rays' situation. That email impressed him, making him want the job even more.

Maddon did his homework, and educated himself on the Devil Rays prior to his interview.

From what he'd gathered, the Devil Rays had played well against the American League West, they seemingly weren't intimidated by American League East teams, and he noticed several pluses and minuses of the team's roster.

Given the fact the Devil Rays had Crawford and Rocco Baldelli, among others, Maddon assessed that the Devil Rays were "among the best in the American League" athletically and that they had an "interesting group of talent."

"I really think back when I first began with the Angels in the minor leagues," Maddon said. "We had a bunch of really good prospects in the mid-80s going into the '90s. Timmy Salmon, Garret Anderson, these guys have the same kind of upside. And having played against them the last couple of years, it's just an exciting group. They're among the best young outfielders in the American League. [Carl] Crawford's already been an All-Star, Rocco [Baldelli] certainly can be one. Guys coming up like Delmon Young, you've got Jonny Gomes, it's a marvelous group of outfielders."

Maddon observed that the team's pitching and defense needed to be improved, and he shared his belief that strong teams had four pitchers in the bullpen who could handle the heat and take the ball when the team was tied or leading late in the game.

"You can sustain a winning streak that way," Maddon said.

The Devil Rays interviewed Maddon twice, and the final decision came down to Maddon and McLaren.

"It was obvious there was going to be a lot of changes in the organization," Topkin said. "The new ownership had taken over. They brought in a new front office of these young kids [and] nobody knew them or what they were going to do, speaking of Andrew Friedman and Matt Silverman. And then as they worked their way down the list of who they were looking at as manager some less traditional concepts [emerged].

"If you looked at the list of candidates, there were some interesting names on there. Ultimately, it kind of came down to an old-school guy and then the opposite of an old-school guy—that's between McLaren and Maddon. I think everyone's first impression of Joe is you're kind of fascinated by him as a person. But boy, he's different as a baseball guy."

After what felt like an eternity to Maddon, a man who'd performed literally every possible job in baseball, he earned his first major league managing job.

The Devil Rays officially announced Maddon as the fourth manager in franchise history during a noon press conference on November 15, 2005, at Tropicana Field.

"I am thrilled to become the manager of the Tampa Bay Devil Rays," Maddon said. "It was an easy decision, made even easier by my comfort with the new front office team. Given the organization's new direction and its talented nucleus, we have the potential to experience great success."

Friedman told the gathering they had been "consistently impressed with Joe throughout our search process."

"Joe brings tremendous energy and optimism to the club-house, and he is respected among players and fellow coaches as a very effective communicator," Friedman said. "His extensive experience on both the major and minor league level will benefit our organization and our players."

Hunsicker, who had participated in the interview process, called Maddon's second interview with the Devil Rays "the most impressive interview I've been through in my career.... He's a very progressive personality."

Upon taking the job, Maddon's priority was to hire a coaching staff.

"I wanted positive guys who are great communicators," Maddon said. "I've always thought about that."

He wasted little time in announcing his staff, which included Mike Butcher as his pitching coach, Bill Evers as bench coach, Tom Foley as third-base/infield coach, Steve Henderson as hitting coach, George Hendrick as first-base/outfield coach, and Bobby Ramos as bullpen/catching coach. Longtime baseball icon Don Zimmer agreed to return to the Rays as a senior baseball advisor.

Maddon noted that his new coaches were "great communicators and great listeners" who interacted well with players.

"I feel this group encompasses all of the qualities that make up a great major league coaching staff," Maddon said.

Butcher came from the Angels, where he'd been a roving pitching instructor for the previous three seasons. Henderson had been the Devil Rays' minor league hitting coordinator for the previous seven years, and had been the team's major league hitting coach in 1998. Evers had joined the Devil Rays organization in 1995 and had spent his entire career at the minor league level. Foley had been the team's third-base coach for the previous four seasons, and had been in the organization since 1996. Ramos had been a minor league manager in the Devil Rays system from 1997 through 1998 and was on the major league staff for a month in 1998. He had spent the previous six seasons in the Angels' organization, including three seasons on the major league staff. Knowing Maddon's history, Ramos called him "very positive" and "very upbeat."

"He has tremendous detail," Ramos said. "He's done everything at every level.... He's an outstanding baseball guy. Tremendous knowledge. He's an awesome guy to work for, very positive, upbeat, and aggressive."

Of all Maddon's coaches, Hendrick owned the best baseball card. He'd played 18 major league seasons. He'd been a major league coach for the Angels from 1998 through 1999.

After spending time assembling his coaching staff, Maddon looked to communicate with everybody in his new world, whether players or coaches. He planned on reaching out and talking with each of them individually.

Looking ahead, Maddon allowed that one of his goals was to create a home-field advantage at Tropicana Field, which he believed should be a given based on the roof, the artificial surface, and the stadium's many quirks. In doing so, he hoped to create a situation where other teams dreaded playing inside The Trop.

Behind the scenes, Maddon and the Devil Rays' front office no doubt knew they did not have the talent to compete. That did not stop Maddon from being a positive voice once spring training opened for the team in St. Petersburg.

In addition to trying to infuse his positive outlook into the negative culture that prevailed in the Devil Rays' clubhouse, Maddon brought a lot of ideas, some of them old school.

For example, he believed in drill work to keep the team sharp.

Fundamental drills such as infielders taking ground balls and outfielders throwing to bases had been around since before Babe Ruth ever swung a bat. While Maddon believed in fundamentals, he believed in a different approach to selling fundamental drills to his team.

Players often perceived drills as punishment. And managers and coaches often served up fundamental drills in response to bad plays that were made in the field. Maddon chose to serve up fundamental drills on a random basis, rather than a response to a mistake or mistakes.

"You need to do the little things properly as often as possible," Maddon said. "It's just how you present it to the guys, you don't present it as punitive. When you spring things on people as punitive that's when you have problems."

Maddon had always been the loyal subordinate. Now he called the shots, and he definitely wasn't your father's manager.

For example, a copy of the book *Blink: The Power of Thinking Without Thinking* sat on his desk. How many major league managers knew who Malcolm Gladwell was, much less read him?

Once the Rays' daily spring training workout ran its course, Maddon would stage his second of two media sessions at the Rays complex in St. Petersburg. Trying something a little different, Maddon gave the sessions a tiki bar feel. A bucket of beer sat on a table underneath an umbrella. Media members were welcome to partake of a beer or two while Maddon talked about everything and anything, even finding time to talk a little bit about baseball. No questions were off limits, and he answered sincerely, even if other reporters had asked him the same question the day before. Never did he go old school by "blowing up" a reporter who had not done his homework, or asked a question most considered stupid. But that was his nature. He respected people, and almost immediately, everyone in the media loved him.

"Joe got it," Topkin said. "This is strictly manager media relations. You could do your job really bad one day, and Joe could make you look really good. Because any question you asked him, he would give you an answer on. He would give you a thoughtful answer to any topic or any question. He didn't just stick to baseball. I can't tell you how many times I walked out of his office and felt like I'd learned something."

Maddon also displayed a humane quality while dealing with the media, which isn't always the case with many managers, who have a low tolerance for questions they deem stupid or out of line.

"One of the things I really liked about him was he could sniff out the one guy in the media scrum who might not have been around too long," said Roger Mooney, who covered the team for the *Bradenton Herald* and later the *Tampa Tribune*. "Sometimes you get somebody out there who hasn't been around much and he or she is really nervous. He could sniff that out and he would put them at ease. When that guy stuttered out his question, he would lock onto him. His undivided attention. He'd give that guy an answer, or lady. He'd give them an answer that would write the story for them. And he knew that. Because I've seen guys who don't want to deal with that."

At the end of the day, Maddon would hop on his bicycle for a 15-mile ride on the Pinellas Trail. Separating himself further, Maddon stressed that he liked to have fun and he wanted his players to have fun, too. Most of all, he enjoyed being unique and didn't feel as though he needed to follow a script established by other managers.

"When you start getting involved and comparing yourself to someone else, that's always dangerous," Maddon said. "I'm not going to be something I'm not. I don't believe in that. I don't want the players to do that. I really don't appreciate people who do that. This is what I am, this is how I am, this is what I have, this is what I believe in."

Being in charge allowed Maddon to focus on some of the things he considered important, like controlling the running game.

"The game had changed a lot," Maddon said.

He remembered baseball in the 1980s, when Rickey Henderson, Vince Coleman, and Tim Raines were stealing bases like squirrels gathering acorns. Teams like the Kansas City Royals dominated on their home fields, and speedy players scorched the base paths. The huge outfields in their home parks embraced that speed, allowing them to run down balls in the gaps. Pitching, defense, and speed characterized those teams.

"With the Cardinals, when Whitey Herzog had the Cardinals, no telling how many bases that group stole," Maddon said. "The Royals. It was a fast-break offense all the time. That's what they were trying to do. They had these big ballparks. Big gaps. They've got fast guys. And they took advantage of it on offense too. I saw it work, so I believed in it."

Maddon foresaw teams with a similar composition coming back into fashion.

"I wanted the Rays to be a combination of speed and power," Maddon said. "I wanted us to be able to hit a three-run homer and create some havoc on the bases. The other team really doesn't like it. Speed, and the threat of speed, upsets the other team because the pitcher doesn't like it, the catcher doesn't like it, the infielders don't like it when there's always pressure on making the throw to first base. And that's the big variable in deference to Bill James.

"I think the game is transitioning back to that type of game. The steroids situation or HGH situation flipped that trend from speed to power for a while in baseball. The coming trend without all of that will be on playing the game properly, where you have to do the little things better, that will become more profound in regard to winning games than the last 10 or 15 years when the home run ruled."

Stopwatches came into vogue since the previous era of speed that preceded baseball's steroids era. Maddon explained how stopwatches were used to try to control the running game.

"You use your stopwatch from the moment the pitcher moves," Maddon said. "That's when the watch starts and it stops the moment it hits the catcher's glove. I'd say 1.3 is average. If you get a pitcher who is 1.2 you have a pretty good chance of throwing out even a good base stealer because average time for a catcher to second base is 2.0. Just say 1.3 for catcher to the plate, catcher is 2.0, that's 3.3 to second base. Now that's just to get there. Now if it's in a bad location, that's not going to help either because it takes longer on the tag. I think 3.3 to the bag you have a pretty good chance to get a good runner with the throw because I used to time Rickey Henderson and some guys with their lead, a guy that can really go is 3.2 or 3.3.

"I'd say it's gotten more intense in regard to trying to stop the running game. Whereas when we study it, we do breakdowns of when every team runs, who's hitting, who's the base runner? The other thing we do, when a manager leaves a ballclub, I throw everything away, all the information. Because a lot of times that footprint is different with a different manager in town. It's just become more sophisticated. There's much more information. Much more is done to try and prevent it. I remember discussions about the free base situation. If you could steal a bag, a free bag during the game, your winning percentage goes up. If you prevent it, you're winning percentage goes up. I want to be on the right track trying to control it."

In addition to the young talent present on the 2006 Devil Rays, with left-hander Scott Kazmir and left fielder Carl Crawford highlighting the group, they had a talented group of players coming up through the team's farm system. Maddon also inherited several disgruntled veteran players, who were less than enamored to be on the Devil Rays and didn't know what to make of their new bespectacled manager.

Still, listening to Maddon talk about his team, one would have thought he had the roster of the 1927 Yankees.

"You look at the major league team itself and there are a lot of talented people," Maddon said. "And you look at the minor league situation. There are a lot of talented people there. You put all this together and there's a lot of good stuff going on here. What we want to do is be able to augment what's been going on."

After getting through spring training and playing their games at historic Al Lang Stadium, which had served as the spring training venue for the New York Mets, St. Louis Cardinals, and Baltimore Orioles, Maddon and the Devil Rays set the team's opening day roster. And while Maddon might have put his best positive spin on it when talking about the group, he had a team that sat on the other side of the spectrum from the 1927 Yankees.

Here's the starting lineup for Maddon's first game as manager of the Devil Rays on April 4, 2006, against the Baltimore Orioles at Camden Yards: Julio Lugo, shortstop; Carl Crawford, left field; Jorge Cantu, second base; Aubrey Huff, third base; Jonny Gomes, DH; Travis Lee, first base; Toby Hall, catcher;

Damon Hollins, right field; Joey Gathright, center field; and Scott Kazmir, starter.

Maddon wouldn't give a specific goal for the season, which he explained.

"Seventy [wins] is not a goal, 81 is not a goal," Maddon said. "Our goal is to play the game properly every night. We're going to aim high. I'm a big reader. I read *Wisdom of the Ages* by Wayne Dyer. It's a collection of 60 short stories. It talks about Michelangelo. Michelangelo aimed high. Look at the history of this man. The David is pretty cool, the Sistine Chapel is pretty neat also. He talks about if you aim low, the concern is that you might hit the mark. So we're not going to aim low, we're going to aim high and see what happens."

Maddon's mother, Beanie, and his sister, Carmine, made the 199-mile trip from Hazleton to Baltimore for their Joey's debut, bringing along hoagies from the Third Base Luncheonette. Maddon teased with reporters that those who visit him from his hometown had to bring either Third Base hoagies, Bellhop's steak and cheese hoagies, Senape's cold-cut pizza, or he would not leave them tickets.

After 31 years, his day had come. He admitted that the day brought him the jitters.

"Because it is what it is, it's the new Rays and we're going to get after it," Maddon said. "We've had a great spring training. I'm really eager for us to get started to see how it all shakes out. I'm big into theory, [but] when theory and reality come together, that's even more fun. So let's see how quickly we can get to that point."

Maddon's first game didn't live up to the sandwiches delivered by his family. A crowd of 46,986 watched as the Devil Rays took a 9–6 loss. Most of the damage came from the three home runs surrendered by Kazmir to Miguel Tejada, Luis Matos, and Melvin Mora. The frustrating part—though Maddon did not show his frustrations afterward—was the fact their home runs had come on counts of 0-2, 0-2, and 0-1, respectfully.

Maddon's second game didn't go any better. The Orioles throttled the Devil Rays and starter Seth McClung 16–6.

On the team's final night in Baltimore, the Devil Rays claimed a 2–0 win to complete the three-game series and give Maddon his first win.

Starter Mark Hendrickson, a 6'9" left-hander who had once played in the NBA, pitched a complete-game three-hitter. The complete-game shutout was the first by a Devil Rays pitcher since Jorge Sosa had turned the trick against the Seattle Mariners in September of 2003.

The complete game prompted Maddon to expand on the benefits of letting a pitcher throw a complete game if he can do so.

"When a pitcher throws a complete game, that does something for him internally," Maddon said. "I believe that. Also, it elevates the team, too.… I'd like to see us try and get as many complete games as we can, even if it means pitching 120, 125, 130 pitches.… As long as [the pitcher is] not coming out of his delivery, and he's not laboring, there's nothing wrong with having him throw a few more pitches. That's going to be the benchmark."

Maddon noted that while in the Angels' organization he'd grown to appreciate what a complete game did for a pitcher.

"They just felt better about themselves," Maddon said. "And we need to elevate our pitchers. It's contagious. Good hitting is contagious. Good pitching is also contagious. Guys want to keep up with the club."

When the Rays finished their six-game road trip to start the season by taking the first and third games in Toronto to claim the series, and move to .500, Maddon invoked an old Meatloaf song into the conversation. "Two Out of Three Ain't Bad," Maddon said. "Meatloafing" an opponent would become a Maddon go-to staple.

At the end of April, the Devil Rays were 10–14 and in fifth place in the American League East. By the end of May, the losses continued to mount. The Rays fell 11 games behind.

Maddon remained optimistic, never beating up his players, choosing instead to continue heaping praise on the group. Behind the scenes, Maddon, Friedman, and Hunsicker were evaluating which players in the group could play, identifying those they wanted to be wearing Tampa Bay uniforms once the tables were turned for the franchise.

Clearly, Kazmir, Crawford, and Rocco Baldelli belonged on that short list. Another player to be added to that list joined the team in May, and made his first major league start on May 31 at Baltimore. James Shields didn't get the win that night, but Maddon and company knew they had something special in the right-hander.

Maddon had seen Shields pitch three games with the Devil Rays in the spring when he held opponents to a .143 average with a 3.00 ERA in his first major league camp. He came away touting how much he liked Shields' makeup and how he'd made the impression that he knew how to pitch, and he threw strikes. In 93 minor league appearances, Shields had a 3.67 ERA, and he'd never had a losing record.

Shields had signed with the Rays out of high school after getting drafted in 2000. He said that the feeling of change being in the air could be felt in the minor leagues the previous season when they began hearing that Sternberg's group was preparing to take over and planned on instituting a new way of doing things.

"The whole message in 2006 was, 'We're going to create a culture, we're going to create a Devil Rays way,'" Shields said. "And that was the Devil Rays way of playing baseball. Joe created that. Not only at the big-league level. But he created that kind of mentality and it went all the way down to the minor leagues. So when guys got called up, they understood how to do things.

"In my view, you had to have veterans in the clubhouse to be able to create that atmosphere. When I got called up in 2006 we had a bunch of guys who were either free agents that year or weren't going to be with the team in the next couple of years, and you could see they were starting the process about who was going to be with the team and who wasn't."

Shields said he "definitely knew" the direction in which Maddon was headed because Maddon would call him into his office during his rookie season and he "challenged me to be a leader."

"I thought it was kind of weird, because I'm thinking, 'Hey I'm a rookie, I'm brand new,'" Shields said. "I had guys around me who had eight to 10 years in the big leagues and he wanted me to be a leader on the team. Then I understood. We had a lot of the chats in the clubhouse, on the field, off the field. I knew what kind of culture he was creating. And I knew what he wanted to do starting then."

Though just 25 at the time, Shields arrived at the major leagues more mature than most rookies. He and his future wife on minor league money, already had a child and they'd survived in the minor leagues on minor league money while raising their child. Shields had also experienced the possibility of having his career end before it ever got started due to shoulder surgery. His first cousin, Aaron Rowand, was a major leaguer and had clued him in on what it took to be a major leaguer. Maddon saw the maturity in Shields and seized the opportunity to enlist a leader in the clubhouse. Shields allowed that he felt lucky that he understood what Maddon was doing from the beginning.

"I was fortunate," Shields said. "When I was in high school, I had a head coach, he was 63 years old, and a very old-school guy. When I played for him, I didn't really understand what he was doing until after I'd played for him. So it was kind of one of those things where I didn't really appreciate him until after I was done.

"When I played for Joe, I appreciated right away, because I understood what he was doing and his philosophy on coaching and things like that. What a brilliant mind he had. He was well ahead of the game, and still is. He's constantly evolving as a coach. And one of the things I loved about him as a player was the fact he allowed us to be men instead of being baseball players, or kids. He allowed our young group to be men and equipped us to do what we were capable of doing and brought us to the ultimate potential that we had as baseball players."

Shields believes that Maddon's approach of letting his team be men made it easy for them to buy what he was selling.

"We bought into the belief that everyone had to believe in each other and the system that he was putting out there, and that was the only way to win," Shields said. "And that went back to creating good chemistry.

"Chemistry is everything to a baseball team, which is something that's getting overlooked more and more because organizations are looking more at the numbers and they don't realize that you can have the greatest numbers team in the world, but if you don't have chemistry, you're not going to win. And he understands that."

When asked to elaborate on what he did that allowed them to be men, Shields said, "We had to be accountable.

"We had to be accountable for each other, teammates," Shields said. "We had to be accountable for our own actions, for what we were supposed to do on the baseball field. He allowed us the freedom to hold each other accountable and to pick each other up. When you do that, you don't have anybody down your throat. When you hold each other accountable, you expect things out of each individual in the clubhouse, and there's really not much to it after that. When you're holding everybody accountable and they know what their job is, it makes the whole season easier. It also gets everybody on the same page and helps them buy into the process that the whole team is working on."

The veterans the Devil Rays needed to move were moved. Dealt by Major League Baseball's July 31 trade deadline were Lugo, Huff, Hendrickson, and Hall.

Minor league shortstop Ben Zobrist was among the players they received in the deal that sent Huff to the Astros. That would prove to be one of the most significant trades in team history.

The Devil Rays clearly wanted to hitch their wagon to young players, and they had enough at the major league level, and coming up through the system, to adhere to that philosophy.

Crawford continued his ascent toward becoming a superstar. In a game in Toronto against the Blue Jays, he demonstrated his immense skills. He went five-for-five, scored five runs, stole four bases, and hit a two-run homer. On July 6, he stole for the cycle against the Red Sox, becoming the seventh American League player to do so since World War II. Crawford's first-ever steal of home highlighted the performance. Crawford clearly had become the face of the team.

Baldelli returned after missing the 2005 season and the first half of 2006 due to injuries.

Kazmir and Shields provided a solid base in the starting rotation.

Kazmir became the youngest pitcher since John Smoltz in 1989 to reach 10 wins by July 3. And he did so by tossing his first complete-game shutout on July 3 against the Red Sox. Meanwhile, Shields got off to a hot start by using a devastating changeup that propelled him to wins in four of his first five starts.

Jonny Gomes gave the team a legitimate power threat. The slugger showed a glimpse of his potential in April when he hit 11 home runs in the month. Down on the farm, top prospect Delmon Young received a 50-game suspension from International League president, Randy Mobley, for an incident that saw Young throw his bat and hit the home plate umpire. Despite Young's apparent anger issues, he joined the team in August, hitting a home run in his first major league game. The Devil Rays eagerly anticipated him having a whole season with the team.

And there was B.J. Upton, an immensely talented player who had been the second player selected in the 2002 June Draft. He entered the organization as a shortstop, but he had not convinced the Devil Rays that shortstop would be his ultimate destination.

The team finished the 2006 season with a 61–101 record, earning the Devil Rays the distinction of owning the worst record in baseball. Not being able to hold leads had a lot to do with that fact. They established an American League record by suffering losses 60 times after having a lead.

Still, optimism ran high within the organization.

"We strongly believe we're in a better place today than we were a year ago," said Friedman at the season-ending press conference.

The fans were buying in, too. The team reported a 20 percent increase in attendance. The Devil Rays had turned Tropicana Field into a home-field advantage, which was reflected in their 41–40 home record.

Maddon noted that what they were trying to do was all "about the process" and by following that process the results would come.

"Things that are worthwhile don't happen overnight," Maddon said. "...No predictions. No promises other than we're going to work the model properly."

Maddon added a message for Devil Rays fans: "Fans, please be patient. Before you know it we'll be playing this time of year instead of watching on television."

The Rays' front office wasn't about to stand pat during the off-season.

They continued to look outside the box by making the winning bid to acquire the negotiating rights to Japanese third baseman Akinori Iwamura. Then they signed him to a three-year, $7.7 million deal with a club option for a fourth year.

Maddon was asked at the winter meetings about the financial disadvantages the Devil Rays dealt with, and how that played in the American League East, which was generally regarded as baseball's best—and richest—division.

"I came into the situation knowing the circumstances, knowing what we are able to do, and I'm fine with that," Maddon said. "That's not my responsibility."

He elaborated by noting that his responsibility was to "take the players that we're given" and try to win with that collection rather than worry about the players they did not have.

"I like the developmental aspects," Maddon said. "I like the fact that you can join a core group together, right here, now. Of course, to augment a situation with a well-chosen free agent or two would be interesting, but for me, I want our guys to understand that this is what we're about. This is where we're coming from. There's no excuses to be made. We know the rules. Everybody plays the same game. So, I'm okay with it. I really am. I find it interesting. I find it a great challenge."

As would be his calling card, Maddon never shied away about playing in the American League East.

"I know, I'm crazy, but I kind of dig the whole scene, and I love playing the American League East," Maddon said. "It's the only place to play. I love the nightly atmosphere when we play the Yankees and the Red Sox and Toronto, and the Orioles. I like it. I really do like it. And I think it's a great challenge for us to compete within this organism, within the parameters that we have set for ourselves."

Maddon allowed that the "one thing I did find out" in his first year was that changing the culture of a team was difficult to do in one year.

"I mean, when you come in and there's people that have been there before and there's different people with different ideas, and I understand that to unfreeze all those items that had been frozen to a certain way and then elicit the change and then try to refreeze things takes some time," Maddon said. "And that's basically what you try to do—try to unfreeze it, make your changes and freeze it back up.

"So, that's what we're trying to get done there. And it really became apparent to me as the season was in progress. Despite all your good intentions and how well you think you laid things out, there's still going to be room where things were misinterpreted along the way. So, as the season was in progress, we figured that out and we got more on board throughout the entire organization."

Ever the optimist, Maddon expected "a lot better cohesiveness" in the 2007 season. And he felt more comfortable entering his second season. As he noted, "I think I have a better feel of what needs to be done and how to approach it."

Maddon had familiarity with everybody in the Angels' organization, building new relationships as they came on a yearly basis. Whereas with the Devil Rays, he had to binge on new relationships. Not only the players he wanted to get to know, but also people in the front office and throughout the organization.

"It is really awkward when you meet people for the first time and you're put in a position of authority and then have to try to determine how this dynamic works here, because I want to be fair to everybody," Maddon said. "But I think after having a year of getting a chance to understand the way this thing works within our group, I feel good about that going into this camp."

Butcher left Maddon's staff to return to the Angels as pitching coach. That opened the door for Jim Hickey to take over the critical position. Otherwise, the staff remained intact.

When camp opened, Maddon harped on controlling the running game and promptly established a dialogue with the pitchers and catchers in the early part of spring training to try and get everyone on the same page. He also arrived with the plan to make Upton into a super utility player, much like Chone Figgins had been when he was with the Angels. Upton would be a familiar site at third base, shortstop, second base, and center field throughout the spring.

Maddon and company were working hard to change the culture of the organization, while also trying to bring in the right players to go forward. Having a little luck didn't hurt their pursuit. Enter Carlos Pena.

Greg Norton went to camp penciled in as the team's starting first baseman.

Maddon liked Norton, who had signed with the Devil Rays as a free agent in January of 2006. He brought with him a veteran presence and he knew how to work at-bats. Playing part time, he went on to have one of the team's better offensive seasons in 2006, hitting .296 with 17 home runs and 45 RBIs.

Unfortunately for Norton, he injured his right knee at the end of spring training, which required surgery, and he hurt his left elbow, which required surgery after the season. Norton's injury came at the worst time for the Rays, and the best time for Pena.

Pena had signed a minor league deal with an invite to the Devil Rays' spring training in 2007. He'd been the Texas Rangers' first pick of the 1998 amateur draft, but he'd never lived up to his potential. He'd bounced around from the Rangers to the Oakland Athletics, Detroit Tigers, and New York Yankees before signing with the Devil Rays.

Pena's power potential and his intellect had always been his best drawing cards. But playing spring training games at spacious Al Lang Stadium didn't help his cause that spring.

"Al Lang was huge, it was right by the water," Pena said. "Even though it didn't get that breezy, it's not exactly a hitter's paradise. My numbers reflected that, no homers, .250, couple of RBIs, hardly an offensive display. I hadn't really done anything special, except maybe Joe thought I had some potential.

He'd seen me in the past and spring training was just spring training."

Prior to the news that Norton had injured his knee, Pena paid a visit to Maddon's office.

"He called me into the office after the final decision has been made that I'm not going to be on the team," Pena said. "He says, 'Carlos, you did a great job.' He was very positive. 'But in reality, we simply don't have enough room for you, so we can't carry you on the team for opening day.' And in that moment, I said, 'Okay Joe, I'm going to go ahead and clear out my locker. But I don't believe what you're saying. I'm going to be in New York on Monday for opening day.'"

Pena laughed telling the story, noting that Maddon had to be thinking Pena was kind of out there.

"Then I told him, 'I've already seen the planes, the planes you see fly by when you're standing on the field for the opening day ceremonies,'" Pena said. "And he's sitting there with a smirk on his face. He's like, *Alright.*"

While Pena weighed his options, his agent called and told him about Norton's injury and that the Devil Rays might be interested in bringing him back. Pena said he slept with his phone that night. The Devil Rays then struck a deal with him that became official two days later.

"I drove back to St. Petersburg from Orlando and walked into the clubhouse," Pena said. "A team meeting is going on when I walk in. I quietly go in on the side and I made my way around the whole clubhouse. And I kind of nodded to all my teammates. Finally, I'm right there with Joe. He wasn't the one speaking. The traveling secretary was making some announcements. And when I saw Joe he was all smiles. When the meeting was over, he came up to me and said, 'When you told me you were going to be on the team, I believed you.' And at that moment, I knew why he smirked."

Pena went on to have one of the best seasons in team history, finishing with 46 home runs, 121 RBIs, 103 walks, 99 runs, and a slugging percentage of .627 while hitting .282. For his efforts, Pena won a Silver Slugger Award and he was recognized as the American League Comeback Player of the Year.

Regardless of Pena's performance, more losing followed in 2007. Still, Pena could feel something special coming together with the Devil Rays, and a close relationship with Maddon was born as well.

"When I first saw Joe, I'm like, *This guy is really cool. Unique.* Starting with his glasses," Pena said. "He was using the thicker framed dark glasses. Those glasses came into style and he was the first guy to wear them. They were nerdy. The black frames. Like you'd see in *Revenge of the Nerds.*"

Pena noticed immediately how well Maddon communicated.

"He had a great sense of humor and [was] incredibly intelligent," Pena said. "I realized he was a leader, and he liked to read. We started talking about books together. All kinds. We exchanged books."

Pena and Maddon had a lot of discussions about Og Mandino's *The Greatest Salesman in the World.*

"We went back and forth about that one," Pena said. "I had recommended that one to him. We talked about *The Art of War* and strategies that we could use, even in baseball. It wasn't just books. I remember him talking about Occam's razor and how you sometimes have a situation and the simplest explanation is the correct one. And how we tend to gravitate toward the more complicated one, even though the simplest one is the correct one.

"All of it was enlightening stuff, and I'm thinking I'm sitting down with a philosopher, who is cool, humorous, and has an electric personality. I just found the perfect combination of a personality. I'm thinking this is the perfect leader here. He's revolutionary, always thinking outside the box. Never conforming to the norm of the moment. I found it really refreshing. It was right up my alley. And we connected that way. He wasn't a follower, he was a trailblazer. And that's what I saw immediately."

Maddon wasn't just Maddon in the abstract, either. Pena enjoyed their discussions about baseball as well.

"The way he talked to me about baseball, nobody had ever talked to me about baseball that way," Pena said. "This is stuff I'd never heard before."

Pena said conversations might take place anywhere, but primarily around the batting cage. In addition to discussions about books, philosophies, and baseball, Maddon talked to Pena about wine.

"I found out he was a wine connoisseur," Pena said. "I'd say, I really like this wine, Joe. And then the next day I found a bottle of wine gift wrapped in my locker. And this is when I'm a bench player and wasn't even starting yet, so he's not trying to suck up to me, I'm not even playing. It's late April in 2007, and I don't think I was even hitting .100. The bottle is an Argentinian blend. I'm like, *This is crazy. Why would he do this?*"

Pena felt special because of the attention Maddon directed toward him. But he wasn't the only one receiving such attention, which amazed Pena.

"I couldn't believe how he seemed to cater to each individual, yet never leaving his principles and ways of thinking and values," Pena said. "But he could relate to every player individually, even accommodating a player's individual interests. He had that type of range, which allowed him to do that."

Like Maddon did with Shields, he encouraged Pena to become a team leader.

"One of the best things I liked about the way Joe ran things is he said, 'I have no rules and if I have no rules, you are going to start taking responsibility and policing yourself. The team itself will take care of its issues,'" Pena said. "When the opportunity came up, I would take the initiative to say to the team, 'We suck, we need to call a meeting. There needs to be a conversation.'

"There were times when Joe would be very strategic. He'd stroll up to me when we were hitting batting practice, and he mentioned one of our players and how he had to dole out some discipline. I told him he'd done the right thing, then I went to the player and we talked. After we talked, we both agreed we'd do certain things together to make sure the issue didn't happen again. Joe would set up a suggestion and I'd take it from there. He'd drop off an observation that would prompt me to lead. Which is kind of cool. Good leaders inspire the people around them to lead. Without commanding, he got the job done."

Pena said the players did not take advantage of Maddon's philosophy of letting the players run their clubhouse for the simple reason, "Joe was respected, but he never demanded respect. He just earned it."

Once again, the July 31 trade deadline brought activity for the team.

They traded former closer Seth McClung to the Brewers for another reliever, Grant Balfour. Former starting second baseman Jorge Cantu went to the Reds for three minor leaguers. And that same day, infielder Ty Wigginton got traded to the Astros for a much-needed setup man, Dan Wheeler. Wheeler and Balfour combined for 47 relief appearances down the stretch and were key pieces for the future.

Pena had 25 home runs by the trade deadline, which made him a target for teams wanting to make a deal with the Devil Rays. While Pena was happy about resurrecting his career, he didn't want to get traded—even if the Rays were in last place.

"I remember going up to Andrew Friedman and to Joe and telling them, whatever you do, do not trade me," Pena said. "They were like, 'You know we're in last place and you're having a pretty good season.' I told them I understood that, but please, 'Don't trade me, I think we're going somewhere.'"

Once the season ended, and Pena had put together what would be his career year, he went to see Maddon and Friedman at Tropicana Field.

"I told them not to be discouraged that we'd finished in last place," said Pena before reiterating what he'd told the pair earlier in the season. "What's happening here is special. I'm telling you there's something special going on here. Something's happening.

"I don't know if they thought I was being grateful or gracious because what had happened to me that season, but I truly meant it. Little did I know we would have such a quick turnaround. It was like a perfect script. I saw it coming. In retrospect, I saw that clearly. And Joe had a lot to do with that."

The Devil Rays losing had its benefits, such as the order they got to select in the draft. In 2007, the Rays had the top pick of the draft and selected David Price, a junior left-hander out of Vanderbilt who had been perched at the top of their draft board since the previous summer. Price signed with the team two months later for $11.25 million over six years. He would quickly become a valuable piece for the team.

The Devil Rays finished strong in 2007—for the Devil Rays.

After experiencing a death march that saw them go 7–20 in July, they went 15–14 in August before finishing with an 11–16 September. After going 34–53 in the first half, they improved to 32–43 in the second half. While the gains were small, the feeling, like Pena said, was that something special was on the horizon.

Baldelli again struggled with injuries in 2007. Given those troubles, Maddon opted to proclaim that B.J. Upton would be his center fielder going forward. Upton had played second base before settling into center field, and he had a nice season, hitting .300 with 24 home runs and 22 stolen bases.

Maddon experienced a major manager moment during the final series of the season against the Blue Jays in Toronto.

Young did not hustle running out a ground ball in the second to the last game of the season and Maddon pulled him from the game, noting that Young had shown a "blatant disrespect" for the game and the team.

After the game, a disgruntled Young told reporters that he was finished for the season.

Maddon and Young hashed out their differences prior to the final game of the season, but Maddon did not start Young, who had played well enough to receive American League Rookie of the Year consideration (though Dustin Pedroia would claim that honor). Maddon had made his point by lifting Young and not starting him, while the punishment was not too punitive. He allowed Young to play in the game. That enabled Young to play in 162 games that season.

Young apologized. In turn, Maddon attributed the sins of his right fielder to his youth.

"And in situations like that, it's almost like talking to your son at that particular age," Maddon told reporters. "You know there are certain things you have to filter through at times. We did. And I told him exactly how I felt again. And by the conclusion of the conversation I was pleased with our conclusion. And we were ready to move on. It's behind us and I never want to see that come up again. It reflects upon the whole organization. There have been so many positives that have occurred of late, I don't want this to be the parting shot for the year."

Young would help the 2008 team win, even though he didn't get a single hit for the team.

Maddon had been at the helm for a lot of losing baseball by the last month of the 2007 season. Any time there is losing, a manager's job can be in jeopardy.

"Oh, I think for sure everybody wondered whether he'd keep his job," reporter Marc Topkin said. "I remember writing that he had a two-year contract with a two-year option. I think that was a very fair question whether they were going to bring him back or not. I think, as a reporter covering the team, that was a big question. Because some of the things he did had worked, and obviously, some of the things he did didn't work. When you're different and you're quirky and you're winning, it's one thing. But when you're different and you're quirky—and I know Joe hates the word quirky—but when it doesn't work, people wonder."

Rumors aside, Sternberg's ownership group, Friedman, and company, were all on board with finishing what they had started. In line with that sentiment, the Rays picked up the two option years on Maddon's contract. The move insured that Maddon would remain manager of the team through the 2009 season. Maddon appreciated the gesture, telling reporters, "I know it's a two-year extension, but I want to be here for years to come."

11

9=8 Magic

AFTER ABSORBING TWO LOSING SEASONS, THE DEVIL RAYS'
new regime was more than ready to turn the page and go for it.

Part of that go-for-it attitude dealt with exorcising the past. That meant re-branding the team, complete with a name change and new uniforms.

They commemorated the change by holding a party at St. Petersburg's Straub Park.

The name change wasn't complicated, they simply dropped the "Devil" from the name, going with a simple "Rays." A bright yellow sunburst icon, to celebrate life in the Sunshine State, accompanied the change.

Navy blue and light blue were adopted for team colors, pushing Devil Rays green to the wayside. Eighteen of the team's players went on stage to model the new uniforms in front of the crowd of approximately 7,000. Former Devil Rays Fred McGriff and Wade Boggs also modeled the uniforms, as did the coaches. Fireworks followed, and actor Kevin Costner and his band, Modern West, entertained.

Carl Crawford could be found among the group, and he was excited about the changes, noting he was the most optimistic he'd ever been while playing for the team.

Stu Sternberg noted they felt changing the team's identity was a must.

"It was something where we were tied to the past and the past wasn't something we necessarily wanted to be known for," Sternberg told MLB.com. "Nobody's running from it or hiding from it, and we're proud of certain aspects of it. This is something the organization has really been able to put their arms around and I'm hoping the fans will see it as a new beginning."

Maddon liked the timing of the changes.

"Because you're always looking for that symbolic moment to really move on to that next area where we want to within the standings, getting to the playoffs, etc.," Maddon told MLB. com. "There are a lot of things coming together at the right time."

Maddon didn't let the losing take him down. The smile never went away.

"I promise, I never despaired in any way, shape, or form," Maddon told the *Tampa Tribune*. "You get your teeth kicked in a little bit, but if you just keep going, there's going to be a nice reward at the end of it."

Changes on the field would soon follow.

On November 28, 2007, Delmon Young and infielder Brendan Harris were shipped to the Twins, along with minor league outfielder Jason Pridie, for right-hander Matt Garza, shortstop Jason Bartlett, and minor league right-hander Eduardo Morlan.

An external factor that helped make the deal attractive to the Twins was the fact their Gold Glove center fielder, Torii Hunter, signed a five-year, $90 million free agent deal with the Los Angeles Angels. That left the Twins with a hole in their outfield. They believed Young could fill that hole.

On the flip side, the Rays were ecstatic with their haul in the deal. Garza had electric stuff. He could be penciled in alongside Scott Kazmir and James Shields in the starting rotation, leaving just two spots open in the rotation for competition. Bartlett brought an immediate upgrade at shortstop.

The next day, the Rays pulled the trigger on a deal to sign veteran closer Troy Percival to a two-year, $8 million deal. The 38-year-old right-hander came out of retirement in 2007 to go 3–0 with a 1.80 ERA in 34 appearances for the St. Louis Cardinals. He'd left baseball due to an injury he suffered while pitching for the Tigers. He missed the second half of the 2005 season and all of 2006 before signing with the Cardinals in June 2007. He'd pitched almost entirely in middle relief that year.

Percival was a four-time American League All-Star, and ranked 12th on the career saves list at the time with 324 in stints with the Angels, Tigers, and Cardinals.

The Devil Rays had dropped 16 games in 2007 after holding a lead in the seventh inning or later, and six times after leading in the ninth. Defying logic, they'd also lost six games after holding leads of five or more runs. Percival's signing appeared to answer the Rays' need for an experienced closer, at least on the surface.

Percival wasn't convinced he could effectively do the job they were hiring him to do.

"I was going to retire," Percival said. "And I told him that. I said, 'Joe, I don't have much left.' But he was persistent. He knew what he needed for a championship team, and not many managers are going to listen to a guy say, 'I don't have anything left' and tell them, 'I don't care if you have anything left.'

"He said, 'Percy, I need you. I need you to come in here and bring my locker room together.' He knows that's something I'd always been capable of doing. He told me, 'This is your strength for me now. It's not 95–97 mph. It's not 40 saves. I need you to come here and get this organization on track.' I trusted him with anything. I would do anything he asked me to do."

In addition to being reunited with Maddon, Percival like the idea of joining an organization that he felt was trying to do everything the right way. He allowed that he did not believe that a team had to have the highest payroll to succeed.

"I'd been a part of something special in Anaheim," Percival said. "We'd won the World Series and we didn't have a payroll that was anywhere close to the highest payroll in baseball."

Once the calendar turned to January 2008, the Rays rewarded Pena with a three-year, $24.125 million deal. Shields then signed a long-term deal for $44 million to possibly keep him with the team for seven years.

They continued to make moves, bringing in Willy Aybar in a trade with the Braves. They also signed veteran free agents Cliff Floyd and Eric Hinske.

When spring training opened in 2008, Maddon wheeled out his slogan for the season: 9=8.

T-shirts were made and he explained to his team the slogan's meaning.

The gist of the formula dealt with having his team purge the past, and to start anew. After being beat down as they had for so many years, the team needed to realize they could play significant games in October. They needed to have nine guys playing hard for nine innings and that would equal one of eight postseason spots.

"The whole point was to just have it out there on a daily basis, so when someone's walking behind somebody, they can see it," Maddon told MLB.com. "We have little signs on the wall, again, reminding. I know a lot of times they will walk by and not focus on it, but sometimes, just for a moment, they will. And the impact of that moment is worth it. That's the way I see it."

Maddon hatched the slogan while on a bike ride.

The slogan, along with Maddon's way, had a profound effect on the team.

"He made us believe," Garza told the *Tampa Tribune*.

Pena remembered the slogan, noting, "It made total sense to all of us. This 9=8 was what any baseball team wants to be."

A unifying moment occurred during spring training when minor leaguer Elliot Johnson flattened Yankees catcher Francisco Cervelli during a Grapefruit League game at Tampa's Legends Field, injuring Cervelli. Days later, Shelley Duncan of the Yankees slid high into Rays second baseman Akinori Iwamura, inciting a brawl at Al Lang Stadium. The way the Rays responded sent a message that the Rays were no longer going to take anything from any team, including the Yankees.

"I don't think the Rays expected to be that good in 2008," Marc Topkin said. "They changed their branding. They went to the Rays from the Devil Rays. They were setting the stage this was going to be a new year. But I think they still thought they were a couple of years away from getting better. I think there was the incident in spring training where Elliot Johnson ran over Francisco Cervelli. [Yankees manager] Joe Girardi said that's not the way you play baseball in the spring. I remember calling Joe Maddon at dinner that night and [I] say, 'Joe Girardi said this.' And Joe's like, 'What have I told you guys all the time? I tell the players I want you to play the same on March 15 as you do on August 15 and October 15, and that was a great example.'

"I think that moment kind of crystalized things for the team. There was some fallout after that. Shelley Duncan went after Akinori Iwamura at second base. And then Jonny Gomes came running in from the outfield, and I think that kind of galvanized the team. I think Joe saw that opportunity there to let the players be themselves and realize, 'Hey we can do something here.' And Joe was a master at letting the clubhouse kind of form it's direction and he'd kind of just push it along. He'd let the players police themselves."

David Price pitched for the Rays during the spring, and opened eyes. He didn't make the team, but he managed to offer the team a preview of the talent waiting to join the team. Everybody who followed the Rays knew the team had a secret weapon in the waiting.

Highly touted third-base prospect Evan Longoria joined the team that spring.

"The one thing that was immediately noticeable with Joe was his ability to connect to the guys and the draw, or the aura, he had in the clubhouse and the ability to capture guys and get a bunch of guys going in the same direction," Longoria said.

Longoria failed to make the team out of spring training. Many players on the team were outspoken about the decision.

Longoria had done everything asked of him and they wanted him to be the starting third baseman.

Grant Balfour did not make the team out of spring, either, much to the Australian-born right-hander's chagrin. He would return with a vengeance and become a critical component to the 2008 team. At the end of March, the Rays had the best spring training record with an 18–8–2 mark.

Kazmir would have been the opening day starter, but he started the season on the disabled list. Shields moved into the top spot and got the decision in a 6–2 win at Baltimore that kicked off the Rays' season.

Hard luck greeted the Rays thereafter. Dioner Navarro sliced two fingers on the dugout netting at Yankee Stadium, sending the team's starting catcher to the disabled list. Aybar, the team's starting third baseman, followed shortly thereafter.

Aybar's injury prompted the Rays to call up Longoria, who made his major league debut on April 12. He led a three-game sweep of the Blue Jays, and when Shields pitched a two-hit shutout over the Red Sox, the Rays had notched their first sweep of the Red Sox in a series of at least three games. The Rays finished April three games over .500, looking as though they might be contenders.

"Joe never asked too much of me," Longoria said. "He never called me into his office to tell me I needed to do more. It's was just the opposite, he'd tell me not to worry because I was one of the youngest guys on the team. 'We're not expecting you to put the team on your shoulders and carry the team.' Nor was I expecting to do that, but everybody has high expectations for themselves. Those were the times when he was really good at pulling those things out, at critical moments. He wouldn't do it all the time, it just seemed like he was really good at picking the right time to give you a message or a short talk to kind of get yourself back going in the right direction. To ensure you knew you weren't alone. It wasn't all on your shoulders."

Having Floyd and Hinske in place as team leaders helped him get adjusted to life in the major leagues.

"I didn't really recognize that as much back then as I do now that I'm a veteran player," Longoria said. "I'm sure that a lot was happening behind closed doors with our veterans at that time. They were perfect for me. They showed me what it took to play in the big leagues every day. I gravitated toward them because I wanted to see what it took to play at this level and all the things I needed to do to do it right. So, whether it was Joe, or Hinske or Cliff. I really was looking for that as well."

Longoria believed from the start that one of the things that made Maddon successful and likeable in the clubhouse was the freedom he extended to his players.

The team continued to play well in May, though they suffered another setback when Troy Percival went on the disabled list.

"Joe knew going in that I just didn't have much left," Percival said. "Day in and day out, he'd ask me what I had left. I'm always the guy, 'Give me the ball, give me the ball.' But every time I took the ball, I got hurt. He knew what was going on. He always stood behind me.

"I enjoyed every day getting to be around Joe. From the minor leagues with the Angels to Tampa. At Tampa, it was hard for me to have a good day since I was hurting all the time and I wasn't a successful player like I'd been in the past. But I still enjoyed going to work every day and being around Joe because of the environment he put out there."

Percival went on and off the disabled list for the remainder of the season. That forced the Rays to turn the closing duties into a group effort.

Fortunately, the Rays had been able to keep Balfour in the organization.

Balfour, who had been designated for assignment at the end of spring training—meaning any team in the major leagues could have claimed him—had re-signed with the Rays. At Triple-A Durham he pitched with a chip on his shoulder, and he became a force, going 1–0 with a 0.38 ERA. He continued to pitch well with the Rays.

J.P. Howell, who had been converted from a starter to a reliever, and Dan Wheeler became a part of the mix as well.

Despite the change from doormats to contenders, Pena remembered Maddon staying the same guy. He recalled a weekday game when he had stayed late at his home at Madeira Beach and cooked out on his deck.

"Then I threw on my sandals and a t-shirt and headed to the ballpark," Pena said. "We had 4:30 stretch that afternoon, and I'm rolling in about 3:45. So I'm late. You want to be there at least an hour before stretch. I'm running, running. As soon as I'm running out the tunnel, I hear the clicking that a bike makes. And it's Joe coming in later than me. I've got sand on my feet still.

"I tell him, 'I'm sorry, I'm late.'

"Joe stops. He says, 'You're not late. You think I want you here two hours early playing cards? I'd rather you be at home spending time with your family.' I could not believe it. I was blown away. But he really meant it. He said, 'What do you think prepares you more, having a nice lunch with your family or being here playing cards for just eyewash?' He was absolutely right."

Still, Maddon wasn't a softie. He wore a different face that he could show when between the white lines.

"One day Victor Martinez was behind the dish and he was complaining about a lot of calls at the Trop," Shields said. "Next thing you know, Joe comes storming out of the dugout and he's yelling at Victor Martinez, out of nowhere. We didn't even know what was happening. He was telling Victor to quit complaining about balls and strikes. Then they get in to it, and the umpires get in to it. There's definitely a tough side to Joe. That's what makes him so interesting. He does have a tough side to him. But a lot of that has to do with him having the players' back no matter what."

The Rays and Red Sox turned into a legitimate rivalry in 2008. As with many such rivalries, bad blood began to brew.

By June, the Rays had swept the Red Sox in three at Tropicana Field, and the Red Sox had swept the Rays in three at Fenway Park. That set up a three-game series at Boston that began June 3.

The Red Sox won the first two games before the finale on June 5, which James Shields started.

In the previous night's game, Red Sox outfielder Coco Crisp went hard into Iwamura at second base. Earlier in that game,

Crisp felt like Rays shortstop Jason Bartlett had blocked the base with his leg when he slid into the bag. That resulted in Crisp injuring his thumb and prompting him to take the action he did.

After the game, Maddon told reporters that Crisp had intentionally tried to hurt Iwamura.

Both teams knew that Crisp would get plunked in the series finale.

Shields understood that doing so would be his duty as the starting pitcher, so he needed to do it the right way by hitting Crisp in the fat part of the leg then moving on. Shields executed his plan, hitting Crisp on the fat part of his leg, but nobody moved on.

Crisp charged the mound, Shields threw a punch and missed, and a brawl unfolded on Fenway Park's manicured infield. The incident led to eight players being suspended, including five Rays.

"The success we had in 2008 began in spring training," Shields said. "We had guys like Jonny Gomes, Cliff Floyd, Eric Hinske, Troy Percival, guys that basically told us in a group that we're not going to take any crap anymore. We're not going to let Boston and New York run all over us like we're their little brother. I think it all started in spring training. We didn't realize how good we were until about two or three months into the season. We really kind of flew from there.

"We had a lot of talent on paper, but it was a matter of how are we going to bring this thing together and how are we going to create a winning culture. When we got into a fight with Boston, we all kind of looked at each other in the clubhouse and we were like, *We're not taking any crap from anybody anymore.* We're going to play as a team and we're not going to back down from anybody. And the cool thing was, Joe had our backs from Day 1."

A buzzkill came heading into the All-Star break.

The Rays held a four-game lead in the American League East before their July 7 game at home against the Royals. They had won seven in a row at that point.

They were trailing 3–2 with one out in the ninth when Carlos Pena hit his 13th homer of the year off a 1-2 Joakim Soria offering. But John Buck answered for the Royals in the 10th, connecting for a three-run homer that hit the left-field foul pole to put the Royals up 6–3. Mike Aviles added a solo homer to complete the Royals' four-run 10th and the Rays took a 7–4 loss. They boarded a charter that night and headed to New York, where the Yankees swept a two-game series—including a 2–1 win in 10 innings on July 9—then they headed to Cleveland to close out the first half before the All-Star break.

The Indians clubbed the Rays 13–2 in the first game of the series, then won the final three to complete the sweep. Andy Sonnanstine took the loss in the first game, then losses by Shields, Garza, and Kazmir followed. All told, the Indians scored 31 runs in four games against the esteemed Rays starters.

In Garza's loss, the Indians built a 7–0 lead after three innings against the right-hander. Afterward, Garza told reporters, "It felt like they knew what I was going to throw before I threw it, 1-2 sliders out off the plate and they were reaching out and shooting them out over the infield. And two-seamers that usually handcuff guys, seeing them spinning on them…. It's real rare for that stuff to happen. I just tip my cap to those guys."

While Garza tipped his cap, he tipped what he thought: the Indians had been stealing signals.

Maddon didn't bellyache about the sweep. The Indians still had to hit the pitches. Accountability directed the Rays to move on, even though they headed into the break in second place, a half a game behind the first-place Boston Red Sox.

At that point, many in baseball acknowledged that the Rays "had been" a nice little story, a real warm and fuzzy tale, but the time had come for the Red Sox to run away and hide.

That collection of Red Sox included Jason Varitek, Kevin Youkilis, Dustin Pedroia, Manny Ramirez, J.D. Drew, and David Ortiz, to name just a few from their star-studded lineup. They easily looked like the better team.

Maddon and the Rays never panicked.

"When we lost the seventh game," Floyd said. "The world is howling, and all he tells us is, 'Enjoy your break. See you in a couple of days.'"

The Rays were still a franchise-best 55–39 at the break, but they needed to get back on track.

Upon their return, Maddon asked his team if they had expected to enjoy a ride to the championship without any bumps. Then he told them that opportunities like the one in front of them did not come along often, so they needed to grab it.

Ben Zobrist led the way in the Rays' first game back after the break. He hit a two-run homer off Toronto's A.J. Burnett in the seventh to give the Rays a 2–1 win. They won their first two series after the break, and suddenly, the skid they'd been on felt like a distant memory.

When August rolled around, the Rays faced more adversity when Crawford, Longoria, and Percival were all lost to injuries. But Maddon successfully mixed and matched his lineups. The results could be seen in the team's 21–7 August record, including a 14–3 win over the Orioles on August 29, which gave the Rays an 82–51 record to ensure the first winning season in franchise history. The Rays held a 5½ game lead over the Red Sox heading into September.

That lead shrunk to 1½ games after a 1–0 loss at Toronto, the day before heading to Boston for a crucial three-game series against the Red Sox.

When the Red Sox won the first game of the series 3–0, most felt like the Rays were finally going to collapse. Only the team once again demonstrated its resiliency, while also re-affirming that they had a little luck on their side as well.

On the morning of September 9, the front office called Jeff Ziegler, the team's traveling secretary, to tell him he needed to get Dan Johnson, Triple-A Durham's first baseman, to Boston for that night's game. The Bulls were in Wilkes-Barre, Pennsylvania, so making said arrangements seemed routine. But weather interfered. Johnson got stuck in the Philadelphia airport. After spending the day in airports, Johnson finally reached Boston about an hour before the start of the second game of the series.

Maddon thought Johnson matched up well against Red Sox starter Daisuke Matsuzaka, so he wanted to start him. But

Joe Maddon grew up in the Angels organization, from Single-A player to minor league hitting coach and all the way up to bench coach for the big club. (John Cordes/Icon SMI)

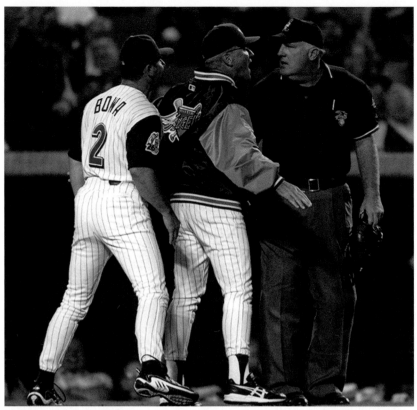

Umpire Larry Young gets an earful from interim manager Joe Maddon in a September 1999 game in Anaheim. (AP Photo/Matt Brown)

One of the best managers of this generation was a virtual unknown as he helped the Angels win the 2002 World Series. But people were starting to notice the bespectacled free thinker. Here he's seen (second from right) during the sixth inning of Game 6 of that World Series, watching the game with hitting coach Mickey Hatcher (center) and manager Mike Scioscia (left). (AP Photo)

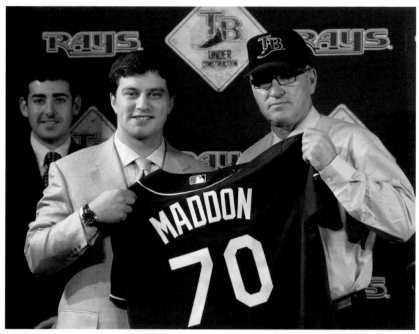

Tuesday, November 15, 2005: Joe Maddon is introduced as the new manager of the Tampa Bay Devil Rays and holds up his jersey with Andrew Friedman, the executive vice president of baseball operations (whose eventual departure to the Dodgers would have surprising contractual significance for Maddon). (AP Photo/Chris O'Meara)

Phillies manager Charlie Manuel shakes hands with Rays manager Joe Maddon before Game 1 of the 2008 World Series. (AP Photo/Chris O'Meara)

Joe Maddon smiles as he address the media before a 2009 game against the Orioles after dyeing his hair black. Road-trip themes have long been a staple of Maddon's. The theme for this road trip was "Cash."

(AP Photo/Chris O'Meara)

Joe Maddon offers to buy a round of drinks at the Cubby Bear after being named the new manager of the Cubs on Monday, November 3, 2014. (AP Photo/M. Spencer Green)

Maddon waits for Jake Arrieta to arrive in the locker room to begin celebrating the Cubs' win in the 2015 one-game Wild Card playoff in Pittsburgh. (AP Photo/Gene J. Puskar)

Maddon greets starting pitcher Kyle Hendricks during the second inning of Game 2 of the Cubs 3–1 series victory over the Cardinals in the 2015 National League Division Series. (AP Photo/Jeff Roberson, File)

October 15, 2016: Joe Maddon shakes hands with Dodgers manager Dave Roberts before Game 1 of the 2016 National League Championship Series at Wrigley Field. (AP Photo/Robin Alam, Icon Sportswire)

After winning the 2016 NLCS and becoming the first manager to guide the Cubs to the World Series in 71 years, Joe Maddon embraces his wife as he gives an interview. (AP Photo/Robin Alam, Icon Sportswire)

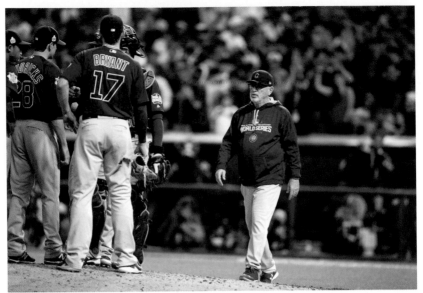

Maddon comes out to pull Kyle Hendricks in the fifth inning of Game 7 of the 2016 World Series. Despite the Cubs' victory, moves such as this would be criticized and scrutinized endlessly after. (AP Photo/Frank Jansky, Icon Sportswire)

Theo Epstein, president of baseball operations for the Cubs, hands Joe Maddon the Commissioner's Trophy in Cleveland on November 3, 2016, after the Cubs won a 10-inning classic against the Indians to end the franchise's World Series drought at 108 years. (Kyodo via AP Images)

after Johnson's late arrival, Maddon told him to hang on for pinch-hitting duties later in the game.

"We all felt like that game was a must win for us," Pena said. "Like if the Red Sox managed to take over first, they would move past us."

Entering the game, the Rays had not won at Fenway Park all season, losing seven times.

"We really had to beat them in their own ballpark to prove to them that we could and to prove it to ourselves," Maddon told MLB.com.

The Rays took a 3–2 lead into the bottom of the eighth only to see Jason Bay, who had been 0-for-18 against Rays right-hander Dan Wheeler, re-route a 1–1 pitch over the Green Monster in left to give the Red Sox a 4–3 lead.

Following the blast, Red Sox closer Jonathan Papelbon entered the game to his familiar music, "I'm Shipping up to Boston" by the Dropkick Murphys.

History suggested the game was over.

Maddon looked to his bench to call on Johnson to pinch hit. Didn't matter that Johnson had an 0-for-15 mark in the major leagues as a pinch hitter, he still was Maddon's guy.

Johnson worked the count to 3–1 then fouled off the fifth pitch he saw, feeling he'd just missed the pitch he'd been waiting for. But he silenced the crowd on the next pitch, connecting with Papelbon's offering and depositing the baseball into the right-field stands to tie the game at four.

The Rays went on to win the game 5–4, and they won again the following night in 14 innings with Pena's three-run homer over the Green Monster leading the way. That gave the Rays their first series win at Fenway Park since 1999. They left Boston with a 2½ game lead.

"Winning that series was huge for us," Pena said. "After that we believed that we could beat them in Boston. That was a powerful thing. Before that series, we had doubts. After the series, we knew what we could do and we felt like Boston knew it, too."

On September 20, the Rays played the Twins at Tropicana Field and came away with a 7–2 win, setting off a raucous celebration as the Rays clinched their first-ever playoff spot.

A week later, the Rays were in Detroit and took a loss to the Tigers. But they didn't go to bed after the game, instead they stayed at Comerica Park to see the end of the Yankees rain-delayed game against the Red Sox. When the Yankees came away with the win, the Rays clinched the American League East and the celebration started.

When the regular season closed, the Rays could look in the rearview mirror and see an improvement of 31 wins from the previous season, which ranked as third greatest turnaround in American League history.

The Rays opened the postseason at Tropicana Field with the Division Series against the Chicago White Sox, and Longoria led the way in a 6–4 Game 1 win with home runs in his first two postseason at-bats. The Rays won again in Game 2 by a score of 6–2, before the series moved to Chicago. Game 3 went to the White Sox 5–3 then the Rays won Game 4 by a score of 6–2 to claim the best-of-five series.

They would see a familiar foe in the American League Championship Series: the Boston Red Sox.

The Red Sox, who entered the playoffs as the American League Wild Card, defeated the Angels to advance. If the Rays were going to reach the World Series, they had to take it to the Red Sox one last time.

After splitting the first two games at Tropicana Field, the series moved to Boston, where the Rays won the first two games by a margin of 22–5. The Rays appeared ready for a cake walk when they took a 7–0 lead in Game 5. But the Red Sox scored four in the bottom of the seventh, three in the eighth, and the game winner in the ninth to take an 8–7 win.

Most figured the historic collapse had thrust a dagger into the heart of the team. But Maddon had conditioned the Rays to handle anything. The constant message preached in the Rays' clubhouse had been to enjoy a win or lament a loss for a half hour after the game, then move on. The postseason seemed to be a different can of worms given the significance of the games. Still, the Rays felt they could put Game 5 behind them.

The series moved back to Tropicana Field for the final two games. The Red Sox took a 4–2 win in Game 6 to force a deciding seventh game.

Maddon didn't appear nervous about Game 7, even though his team would be facing its first elimination game of the postseason.

He told reporters prior to the game, "At this particular juncture for me, I'm just sticking to the overall philosophy of what we've been doing."

Maddon elaborated by noting that for him, it was all about doing things the right way.

"I don't think any kind of speech from me is going to make any difference in tonight's game," he said. "I believe that. I believe us coming together and staying together and keep doing the things we've been doing all year is going to get us to win this game tonight. It's not going to come through words. I think sometimes that's misinterpreted."

The Red Sox entered the game having won nine straight American League Championship Series elimination games. In addition, they were the reigning world champions. The Rays were the "Little Engine that Could."

Maddon summed up his pregame remarks by telling reporters, "I'm really looking forward to it."

"Game 7 of anything is absolutely the most fun it could possibly be," Maddon said. "When you're a kid growing up you're always playing Game 7, so here it is. To be one game away from the World Series, let's go back to the first day of spring training, and if I had told you guys we were going to be one game away from going to the World Series, all of you would have laughed. Absolutely, a good belly laugh.

"I'm very proud of where our group is at today, and I could understand why you would have belly laughed back then. But nobody is belly laughing right now. And I could not be more proud of this group and I have a strong conviction and belief that we're going to get it done tonight."

During batting practice, Maddon walked the outfield, talking to players as he went. David Price was among the players he spoke to.

"I was just out there shagging and he asked me how I felt," Price said. "Joe always said be ready for any situation. So he tells me to be ready. That was that."

Garza pitched a gem, and Price, who joined the Rays' bullpen for the postseason, picked up the save, striking out J.D. Drew to escape a bases-loaded jam in the eighth. In the ninth, he got the final out, getting J.D. Lowrie to ground to Iwamura. The Rays second baseman stepped on second base for the force, and the final out of a 3–1 win.

"I wasn't surprised that he used me in the eighth," Price said. "I guess I was probably a little more surprised that after I got Drew, I got to the dugout and Joe's like, 'You're still going.'"

The Rays were headed to the World Series.

In a year, Maddon had gone from the non-conformist manager with the funny glasses, to manager of the American League champions, and resident genius.

"It's amazing," Maddon said. "I've still got the funny glasses, but it's different because you win. Everything changes because you win. All the things we're doing this year we did a lot of the same stuff last year. Of course, the difference is personnel. You're getting performance. The manager has nothing to do with it.

"You look at the bullpen, you look at the team, you look at the quality of our players, you've got young guys figuring things out. We've been trying to put these concepts out there for the last three years, but it takes time. You just don't get it done overnight."

The Rays met the Philadelphia Phillies in the World Series. After splitting the first two games at Tropicana Field, the series moved to Philadelphia where the Rays dropped the first two games before they took part in a bizarre Game 5, which featured a two-day rain delay before resuming and seeing the Phillies win to become World Series champions.

Ever the half-a-glass-full person, Maddon found perspective, and a happy spin afterward.

"This has been a remarkable year for us on so many different levels, to get to this point," Maddon said. "Very few people in this country or throughout the baseball world would have even guessed that we could get here. I'm very proud of our guys as a group. Really a truly remarkable job. We made a powerful statement. It's just the beginning."

After the season, Maddon married his longtime sweetheart, Jaye Sousoures. The newlyweds honeymooned in Europe, and Maddon was named American League Manager of the Year.

12

Handling Success

UNLIKE MADDON'S PREVIOUS SEASONS MANAGING THE RAYS, he arrived at spring training in 2009 with a team that no longer flew under the radar. As American League champions, they were now the hunted rather than the hunters.

Maddon embraced the difference, telling reporters that he loved being the favorites. "It's much better than being a non-target."

One of his first objectives of the spring was to tell the team that any pressure they might be feeling was self-inflicted and that by supporting each other they should be able to control their emotions. As for expectations, he told the team nobody's expectations for their performance should be higher than their own.

Maddon did allow that he experienced a refreshing change when he mentioned the prospect of playing meaningful games in October and nobody rolled their eyes.

Personally, Maddon didn't feel as though there had been too many changes in his life.

"You get recognized a little bit, and that's nice," he said. "But I still have my same routines."

Maddon maintained the winning wouldn't change him a lot.

"I'll be on the bike and I do my workout routine, and I like to read," Maddon said. "And I get to travel a little bit more, but nothing has really changed for me, quite frankly.

"I know what I like to do, and all this other stuff is kind of cool, but it doesn't really impact me a whole lot. I mean, I like being a baseball manager for the Tampa Bay Rays and I feel very fortunate about our success."

Maddon might not have felt the differences, but Pena said Maddon had to deal with a lot after the Rays' 2008 success.

"I think Joe himself would tell you 2009, 2010 were kind of difficult for him," Pena said. "The stuff on his plate was greater, the expectations were greater. I think he'd be the first to tell you, 'I could have done this, this, and this differently, or that differently. I didn't have to live up to anybody's expectations. I let it put a weight on me.'

"I think Joe was smart enough to know that. I know in 2009, 2010, I put more pressure on myself, I carried more on my shoulders, thinking to myself I was more important than I was. It's not a criticism, it's more of an observation. I know Joe felt that way, too. All of a sudden, he's Joe Maddon, and 'I'm known for my way of leading. I'm known for the way I relate to players. I'm known for how I think so much outside the box. And now here's what people expect from me.' So I know he had somewhat of a struggle there."

While the Rays looked like a better team heading into 2009— at least on paper, that didn't turn out to be the case.

Unfortunately, some of the reasons for the Rays to be optimistic for improvement in 2009 didn't come to fruition. Most notably, Pat Burrell, whom the Rays signed to a two-year, $16 million deal to be the team's DH. The veteran bat came up short of expectations, as did others.

The team got off to a 9–14 start and never recovered.

At the end of the season, Maddon allowed that the lesson learned was that his team needed to get off to a better start, because chasing from behind all season was exhausting.

The Rays finished July six games behind the American League East–leading Yankees. By the time the calendar turned to September, the Rays were out of the running for all intents and purposes. At least that seemed to be the view of management when they traded left-hander Scott Kazmir to the Angels for minor leaguers on August 28.

While the Rays had followed their championship season with a plus .500 campaign at 86–76, they never produced the chemistry to bring about a magical season.

Pena believes the 2009 season "probably gave Joe a learning moment."

"This is my observation," Pena said. "Success has a way of clouding a human being. You have to offset success with a very substantial shot of humility.

"It was almost impossible to replicate the feeling we had in 2007. That mentality was not one we arrived upon by choice. It was a matter of circumstances. We were a last-place team in 2007. So in 2008, we were in a position where our mentalities, we had these beginning minds. These humble minds. Kind of like something that can't be duplicated."

Then the Rays went to the World Series.

"And we weren't the worst team in baseball; we were one of the best teams in baseball, and I'd argue we were the best team in baseball, we just didn't win the World Series," Pena said. "And then we go into 2009 as one of the best teams in baseball, totally different. Now you have to, by choice, seek the beginner's mind. Be disciplined enough to keep the beginner's mind, and be humble enough to keep that beginner's mind. And I think that was where Joe was mostly challenged. Because now he has to manage, or lead, from a position of power or influence that he didn't have prior to that moment, prior to the World Series."

Maddon had gained in popularity. He easily ranked as the favorite manager by baseball writers around the American League because he took time to know all the writers, and always tried to be obliging when giving well-thought-out answers to questions. And he continued to try to relate to his players, getting to know as many of them as possible in a deeper way than baseball.

"Early on, we just talked baseball," Evan Longoria said. "What he could give me, what little bits of advice, game notes or whatever it was. As a young player, you're looking for those things. And it seemed like he could pick whatever it was specifically that was either eating at me, or certain things I could do to make some changes. He was really good at picking those things and just kind of laying them out there for a young player to understand. And then as we got further down the road, I think we had a really good working relationship.

"I felt like he never forced me to try and be a player that I wasn't or didn't expect myself to be. Just really had the ability to calm me down when things got out of control. We both loved cars and we talked about cars from time to time. And we would click with reading. He was probably the first baseball guy that I really talked to on a different level, whether it was about books or the cars or about something that happened on a TV show, whatever it was. There were a lot more conversations probably than things outside of baseball that interested us versus just coming to the ballpark every day and talking about what we're going to do in the game that night."

Obviously, Longoria was one of the best players on the team—if not the best—so he was going to be treated well. But Maddon treated his other players well, too.

Randy Choate joined the team in the spring of 2009 as a non-roster invitee to camp. The veteran left-hander praised the way Maddon and his staff treated him.

"They called me in at the end of spring training and told me they liked what I was doing, but I wasn't going to make the team," Choate said. "They told me I was the first guy they would call if something happened, though. I really appreciated them being up front with me."

Choate said he had an out clause in his contract at the end of May, but he really hoped it would work out with the Rays, "Because I really liked the way they'd treated me."

The Rays had signed southpaw Brian Shouse to a deal worth $1.55 million prior to the 2009 season, which was part of the reason Choate did not make the team and got re-routed to Triple-A Durham. Maddon and the Rays were true to their word. When Shouse went on the disabled list in May, Choate joined the team on May 25 and made 61 appearances in the final 115 games of the season.

"Joe showed a lot of confidence in me," Choate said. "I don't think I ever had a manager that showed as much confidence in me as Joe did."

Typical of Maddon, he gave all credit to Choate, as he told MLB.com: "He threw strikes and when he came up he was a strike thrower. We gave him some opportunities [in 2009] and you could see him start to settle down into it. I liked the idea [that] he threw strikes and was putting the ball into play. And it really became obvious lefties were having a very hard time against him. He's a pro. He does his work. He really fits in well with us. But he threw strikes. It really came down to that. It's still the best pitch in baseball."

Maddon always seemed to be on the lookout for the next new or fun thing for his team. Themed road trips personified the fun.

Players would dress up a certain way depending on the city they were traveling to, or the time of year it was, or for any number of reasons.

Over the next several years, the following themed road trips took place under Maddon's watch: Johnny Cash (all black) to Toronto, accidental preppies to Houston, camouflage to Baltimore, Woodstock wardrobe to Seattle, team lettermen jackets to Boston, hockey jerseys to Toronto, grunge look to Seattle, all-white attire to Miami.

"The themed trips and the silly stuff, it was, I think more bigger picture," Longoria said. "It was more about letting the guys feel a little bit of freedom around the clubhouse. And, also to take your mind off the game of baseball and just free your-self up to be the best player that you could be because I think he really understood how tough it was to play the game every day. Losing five or 10 in a row, or just going 0-for-20. And he always seemed to be able to find a way. I think that was his best tool. And his best tool over the course of his managerial career, just getting guys to do their own thing so they can go out and free themselves up to play the game."

Maddon also showed a human, caring side, like "Thanksmas," an annual holiday tradition when he pulled out family recipes and cooked for those less fortunate.

"You see guys who do these things around the holidays, and they hand out presents or meals or something like that," Roger Mooney said. "He'd cook the meal. Really took pride in cooking the meal. He'd always start off when everybody came into the room, the people at the shelters or the Salvation Army, and he'd say, 'If you enjoy what you're eating, let me know. If you don't, keep it to yourself.' He said it every time, but you laughed every time."

Mooney noted that Maddon never acted like he was better than those he served because he was better off in his life.

"He would talk to people, he would ask them their names, refer to somebody by their name," Mooney said. "And a lot of these people might be sleeping on the street. Don't have a penny to their name. And he's taking the time to address like they're on the same level. I'd cover those things. And you'd wonder, *Where's Joe?* And he's in a corner talking to one or two guys, just sitting there talking to them like they were men. He'd be asking them about their backstory. And not like, 'How'd you end up like this?' Might be the only time in a while they've had a real conversation with anybody as they're struggling to get back on their feet."

Maddon was touched by the story of John Challis, a Pittsburgh teenager battling cancer whose own personal philosophy of optimism inspired so many in baseball. Maddon actually got to meet Challis before the teen died of cancer in 2008, and Maddon was affected by their brief time knowing each other. Maddon would wear a red bracelet that had "Courage + Believe = Life" on it. That had been Challis' motto.

He also became passionate about bringing together the people of Hazleton. During one of his visits home, he noticed palpable tension between the town's older white community and its Hispanic community, which had grown immensely. From that awareness, plans for the Hazleton Integration Project were drawn up. The plan brought about a community-based program in his hometown that sought to unite the cultures calling Hazleton home. The mission statement was to promote positive relationships with the Hispanic population through community activities.

Despite what happened in 2009, Maddon and the Rays felt as though they had the players in place to make another playoff run in 2010. That assessment proved to be correct.

The Rays cruised to a team-record 20 wins in the spring, then got out of the gate quickly to start the season.

Evan Longoria personified the Rays' interest in getting off to a quick start with an opening day 473-foot bomb that landed in Tropicana Field's left-field upper deck, making him just the second player to do so.

The team gave Maddon just want he wanted, a 17–6 start.

Ironically, as good as the Rays were playing, they had a perfect game thrown against them—for the second year in a row. Mark Buehrle of the White Sox had done it back on July 23, 2009, then Dallas Braden twirled the 19th perfect game in major league history on May 9, 2010, against the Rays in Oakland.

Former Rays right-hander Edwin Jackson then tossed a no-hitter against the Rays on June 25 at Tropicana Field, making the Rays the first team to get no-hit twice in the same season since the 2001 San Diego Padres.

Maddon managed to find some humor in the aftermath of Jackson's no-hitter. He learned about Pants Rowland's story and placed a framed a picture of Rowland on his desk for all to see. Rowland had managed the 1917 White Sox, and they owned the distinction of being the only team to reach the World Series after getting no-hit twice in the same season.

Later in the season, Maddon organized a themed road trip in Rowland's honor when they traveled to New York: "The Loudmouth Pants Rowland Trip."

The Loudmouth brand helped facilitate the trip. They made outlandish golf pants, so they sent along pants for everyone in the Rays' traveling party to wear.

A no-hitter finally went the Rays way on July 26, when Matt Garza threw the first no-hitter in Rays history in a 5–0 win over the Detroit Tigers at Tropicana Field.

Kelly Shoppach joined the team prior to the start of the 2010 season. Hailing from Texas, the veteran catcher had a football mentality, and thrived on coaches and managers who were black and white and adhered to discipline. That made Maddon different in Shoppach's eyes.

"My initial impression was, 'Man, what a hippie,'" said Shoppach, who is now a coach at Texas Wesleyan in Fort Worth, Texas. "It's odd, I played for Eric Wedge. He's such a nose to the grindstone baseball, day-round, year-round, the grind, the grind, the grind. Then when I get with Joe, he's rolling in in flip flops. And that was odd for me.

"Wedge's way, with his straight-laced background, made me feel more at home. And that's why I ended up playing for him again in Seattle. He's right up my alley. I was ready to run through a wall for him after his motivation speech. Joe just has a different approach. It's funny, Joe and I might not have seen eye to eye on some things, because there were times when I wanted a straight forward, in-your-face type, and Joe's not that way. But now I'm coaching and I find myself being more like Joe Maddon. It's a little more laid back."

Shoppach eventually saw that Wedge's way and Maddon's could both work.

"The unwritten rules of the clubhouse, I figured out, that really doesn't matter what you wear to the park," said Shoppach, pointing out that with the Rays' budget and all of their young players, Maddon figured he needed to let his players be as comfortable as possible. "So a strict dress code and all that stuff…. Just let them be them. As soon as they get comfortable, they can help us win ballgames."

Shoppach concluded that the players on the Rays needed that comfort level.

"We were a bunch of journeymen, nobodies, with the exception of Longoria and some of those pitchers, obviously, they were dynamite," Shoppach said. "The rest of the lineup was just a bunch of guys he figured out a way to get the most out of them. Whether it was him or just us being able to be relaxed knowing that he had confidence, and that rubbed off on us. For a guy who was a low .200 career hitter, I felt like I was Babe Ruth every time I stepped into the box. I think a lot of that was his belief in me, whether it was deserved or not."

Shoppach pulled up short of anointing Maddon a genius, but he conceded, "He did have a way of making me feel like a confident player."

"My play was not indicating I should be hitting in the three hole in any game—ever," Shoppach said. "But Joe did some goofy things, that were kind of outside the box. Maybe it worked, maybe it didn't. I gained confidence in knowing that the guy in charge had confidence in me. Why in the world wouldn't I have confidence in me? In this game, offensively, once your confidence goes, you're done. If you don't feel like you're going to kill that pitcher every time in the box, you're not getting a hit.

"Joe was always our biggest fan. Whether he really was or not, he didn't show it. You never felt like, 'Oh man, the manager's mad at me, I'm not going to get to play.' At least from my perspective. And maybe that's because he had no choice, he had to play me. But I just felt like he was my biggest fan and he was behind me 100 percent. He was just so enthusiastic about all of us, and even though there were probably a million things going on in Joe's mind, I always felt like he was behind me and really believed that I would get it done. In turn I believed I would get it done, even though 80 percent of the time, I didn't."

On September 28, the Rays clinched a playoff spot when they beat the Orioles 5–0 at Tropicana Field. Then, on the final day of the regular season, the Rays beat the Royals in extra innings to clinch their second American League East title.

Unfortunately for the Rays, the Rangers eliminated them in the Division Series, leaving Pants Rowland's World Series distinction intact.

The Rays dropped the payroll after the 2010 season.

Carl Crawford left the team via free agency for the Red Sox, and closer Rafael Soriano signed with the Yankees.

The Rays' payroll went from $72.8 million in 2010 to $42.1 million in 2011. Meanwhile, the Yankees payroll rested at $207 million and the Red Sox were at $163.8.

Hoping to patch up their roster, the Rays signed veterans Johnny Damon and Manny Ramirez, who had both seen better days.

After losing their first three games of the season to the Orioles, the Rays dropped their next two to the Angels before hitting the road to play the Chicago White Sox.

Shoppach remembered the way Maddon remained calm, pouring his players a shot on the airplane, telling them they were the best 0–5 team in baseball.

"Not that the shots did anything," Shoppach said. "It just let us know it's okay. And we ended up being okay."

Upon reaching Chicago, the team announced that Ramirez had tested positive for a banned performance-enhancing drug. Rather than take the resulting suspension, Ramirez opted to retire.

The Rays then lost their first game in Chicago.

"My mom called me," Roger Mooney said. "She never calls me on my cell phone. I'm like, *What's going on here? Mom's calling me.* I called her back, and she said, 'Oh, the Rays are going to win tonight. I stopped by church and lit a candle for the Rays.' So that's the night they win their first game of the season. After the game, we were talking to Maddon. Once everybody walked out of the room, I waited around and told Joe my mother had said they would win because she'd gone to church and lit a candle for them. He's like, 'Oh, man. What's your mother's name?' I told him, 'Margaret.'

"Next day I'm standing in the clubhouse and he walks by. I've got a coat on and I feel him put something in my pocket. He said, 'That's for Momma.' I waited until I was out of the clubhouse and I looked at it. He wrote: 'Margaret, thanks for the prayers, we need them.' Every year since, my mom has put it out on her old sewing machine table at the start of baseball season."

The Rays' six-game losing streak proved to be the team's last losing streak of more than three games. They would put together six five-game winning streaks, four of which came in the final two months of the season, which fueled an epic end to the season.

Entering September, the Rays were in third place, nine games behind first-place Boston, and 7½ behind second place New York in the American League East.

Maddon told his team they didn't have to make up the difference all at once, suffice it to say, they just needed to gain a little ground each week. Riding that mantra, the Rays went 17–10 in September, while the Red Sox went 7–20.

The final days of the season, the Rays reached deep into their pocket of miracles and found the magical pixie dust.

On September 25, Ben Zobrist hit an inside-the-park homer, just the 10th in team history, to lead a 5–2 win over Toronto.

In the Rays' 161st game of the season, they escaped a jam by turning the third triple play in team history en route to a 5–3 win over the Yankees. That meant the Rays and Red Sox were tied for the American League Wild Card spot heading into the final game of the season.

On the final night of the season, the Rays trailed the Yankees 7–0 after seven innings. Then came the comeback. Longoria's three-run homer capped a six-run eighth inning that left the Rays a run behind heading into their final at-bat. The Yankees were one strike away from winning the game when Dan Johnson homered on a two-out pitch to tie the score, sending the game into extra innings. On the scoreboard, they watched as the Red Sox lost to the Orioles. Then they claimed an 8–7 win when Longoria connected for a walk-off homer moments later.

That game came to be known simply as "Game 162."

"When we did make the playoffs, Joe brought up the beginning of the season in the team meeting after we had that amazing comeback to get it done," Shoppach said. "He said, 'Look, I told you guys back in April we'd be fine.' And we were. It was just that kind of long-term belief and long-term confidence that we fed off…. It's such a unique style. And it was always calm and relaxed, and whenever there was trouble, we'll be fine."

The Rays entered the playoffs possessing a special weapon in Matt Moore, who had joined the team from Triple-A Durham on September 12. The left-hander had what insiders were calling "easy gas," as his fastball registered at 97 mph, seemingly without any effort on his part. In a September 22 game at Yankee Stadium, Moore struck out 11 in a five-inning, scoreless appearance against the Yankees. Moore looked like a phenom. Still, he was a rookie. He'd barely experienced the major leagues, much less the postseason.

Maddon decided he would be the guy starting the Rays' first playoff game against the Rangers.

"Joe had his stat book, but he also had his gut feelings," Shoppach said. "Before that game, Joe said, 'This is what I think is right. And I'm going to run it out there.' And that was Matt Moore starting Game 1 of the playoffs. I'm like, *How do we throw a rookie out there in that sort of atmosphere? Holy crap, what's going to happen?* But Joe has that way of making you feel like you're the greatest player on the planet. He sent him out there, and he dominated."

Moore gave up just two hits in seven innings, striking out seven, and the Rays beat the Rangers 9–0 in Game 1. The Rangers then won the final three games to once-again eliminate the Rays from the postseason.

Maddon and the Rays went to the playoffs one more time in his final three seasons managing the team when they won eight of their final 10 games in 2013 to force a one-game playoff with the Rangers.

And finally, the Rays came up victorious against the Rangers to advance to the Wild Card Game in Cleveland against the Indians, winning their third game in four days in three different cities.

The Red Sox were next in the Division Series. The Rays managed to win just once before getting eliminated by the eventual World Series champions.

Little went right for Maddon and the Rays in 2014, even though they had the look of a team that would contend given their starting staff of David Price, Alex Cobb, Matt Moore, Chris Archer, and Jake Odorizzi, who joined the group after Jeremy Hellickson's elbow surgery in January.

More injuries followed.

Moore made two starts before having Tommy John surgery. Cobb suffered an oblique strain on April 12. The Rays were 7–5 at the time, and the Rays went 12–23 in his absence.

When the Rays reached 24–42 on June 10, they owned the dubious distinction of having the worst record in baseball. They would enjoy a 37–19 run from June 11 through August 15 that put the team at .500 with a 61–61 mark.

That run included a road series against the Cubs in Chicago. During that stay, Maddon seemed to glow in the Wrigley Field atmosphere.

"It's very, very cool," Maddon told reporters. "I'm excited about it. I've never been here before. First time. I've ridden my bike around here in the past. I watched it on television growing up. It's my 20th year in the major leagues and it's my first visit here. I love it. It is the essence of baseball. You talk about Fenway, and what that's all about. The way this is more of a neighborhood setting than Fenway it's uniquely cool. So it's pretty impressive."

Nobody knew how enamored Maddon was with Chicago at the time.

Meanwhile, the Rays couldn't maintain their pace. They finished August at 13–16 and September at 11–14.

"You utilize a lot of mental energy as much as anything to get yourself back [in] there," Maddon told reporters at the end of the season. "And it's not easy to do that. You get back there and you have to maintain this real high level of success on a professional level against professionals. So it's not easy to do. But I really thought we could. I never thought that we could not.

"And all of a sudden, we were on the verge of pulling it off. We got back to .500 and since then it's just been teetering back and forth. Just could not get back to that level of play that we had going on for a long time. It's not easy to do. I understand that."

Maddon had signed a three-year extension with the Rays worth $6 million that would take him through the 2015 season. Prior to the Rays' final game of the 2014 season, Maddon talked to reporters about his status and whether he'd sign another extension with the team.

"I can easily see myself managing for another 10 years," said Maddon, noting that if he wanted to do so, he would need to take care of himself physically.

"Talk about diet, talk about rest...those are the components I need to do these for several more years," Maddon said. "That's what I intend to do. We'll see how the contract situation works out. I love being here. I always want to be here. But I truly believe it's up to me to take care of myself to reach my goals."

At that juncture, he did not make any comments about wanting to have a deal by the following spring training. In short, he seemed perfectly content to be the Rays' manager for the remainder of his career.

"I believe organically the right thing will occur," Maddon said. "I place my faith in that. The people I work with, the people I trust, I put my faith in that area."

The answer whether Maddon would remain with the team came sooner than Rays fans expected. Shortly after the end of the season, the news came out that the Rays executive vice president of baseball operations, Andrew Friedman, left to take a lucrative deal to become the Los Angeles Dodgers president of baseball operations.

Friedman's move clicked into place an opt-out clause in Maddon's contract. Given the opportunity to explore other options, Maddon exercised that clause, which made him a manager free agent, thereby ending his days as the manager of the Tampa Bay Rays.

Mark Topkin, who's covered the franchise since its inception, didn't think Maddon was going to leave the team, not at that point anyway.

"The vibe I was picking up was that he wanted his next contract to reward him for the success he had and the fact that he managed with a somewhat under market contract compared to the bigger name manager," Topkin said. "Which, granted, he wasn't initially. I didn't think he'd leave. I thought he probably would not sign a new deal and then at the end of his contract leave. So I thought he'd spend one more year with the Rays then leave. My vibe was he was expecting to be rewarded with his next contract for what he considered past sacrifices along with past successes."

Evan Longoria referenced a comment made at one time by former major league manager Tony La Russa, who noted that the "tenure for a big-league manager is eight years."

"You kind of wear out your welcome at that point," Longoria said. "And it's kind of funny and ironic, but true. Very few last longer than eight.

"I think Joe leaving was more shocking than anything because we didn't have too many bad years with him. But I think maybe he felt that way too, that it was time to kind of bring what he brought as a manager to a fresh environment, and there's nothing wrong with that. I think from time to time, we all feel that, whether it's your job, or where you live, or what you're in to. Things change, mindsets change. And whether it was something that happened between him and the front office or his views were changing or he just wanted to be somewhere else, who knows. I think it happens over time with everything."

When asked if he thought Maddon's shelf life had expired, Alex Cobb noted, "I'll say this. It's hard to stay creative for that many years. First of all, it's hard to be creative for one year. And to run that out with all the attention it got every single day in the clubhouse, and in the media. It's impressive the way he was able to keep things fresh. I won't say it ran its course, but I'd just say how impressive it was he was able to keep it fresh for so long."

13

Shot and a Beer

IN THE FALL OF 2014, WRIGLEY FIELD HAD BEGUN A MUCH-NEEDED and anticipated renovation project, so when the Cubs wanted to introduce their new, charismatic manager to an excited fan base they had to find a different venue. A month later they would hold a news conference for free agent signee Jon Lester at a swanky downtown restaurant named Spiaggia. They would use the same venue after outfielder Jason Heyward signed on during the next off-season. But Spiaggia was just too fancy for the self-described "shot-and-a-beer" guy Maddon. At least that's how the story is told in hindsight, though the Cubs insist they had Maddon's personality partly in mind when choosing the venue.

Team brass landed on the Cubby Bear, an establishment located kitty corner to Wrigley Field, just steps from the stadium's marquee. It's the quintessential shot-and-a-beer joint, right down to the sticky floors. Fans had been congregating at the Cubby Bear before and after Cubs games for too many years to remember, and it fit right in with the laid-back style of the new skipper.

"When Theo told me we were going to the Cubby Bear and then he described the Cubby Bear to me, I thought, *This is absolutely perfect*," Maddon said. "I knew that would permit me to relax even more.

"I thought, *Man, this is like being back home.* Then we walked in the back door and it had the familiar bar-room smells."

Maddon often says he enjoys a bar-room argument as much as the next guy. Now he was sitting in a place where his decisions would undoubtedly be second guessed from that moment until he was done managing the team. It was the appropriate room for the man that didn't even wear a tie to the White House after winning the World Series.

"All I remember is we didn't have a function room that size, because of all the renovations that were going underway," Theo Epstein said. "We talked about maybe doing it back where we did Lester's, but that seemed a little…I don't want to use the word 'stuffy' because it wasn't, maybe overly formal for Joe. and then we had the idea of one of the local bars and when I threw that out to Joe he seemed pretty excited about it for obvious reasons."

Jed Hoyer thinks the team got lucky, as only later did he fully realize what a perfect venue the bar was for Maddon.

"I think it fit his personality, but we didn't know him as well at the time," Hoyer said. "I don't know if other venues were even an option. It was just born of necessity. We had no place to do a real press conference."

Cubs PR maven Peter Chase had no issues with the optics of being at a bar while holding a formal press conference. After all, how formal was it if the guest of honor would be dressed more as a patron of the bar than that of the keynote speaker?

"The first time I spoke to Joe he asked me what he should wear to the press conference," Chase recalled. "I said how about a suit jacket and slacks and his answer to me was 'What are slacks?' Once he gave me that answer I figured the Cubby Bear would be the perfect place."

Perhaps Hoyer and others within the Cubs who didn't know Maddon realized they had the right man—at the right place—about the time everyone else realized it, once Maddon started talking. He won the room over pretty quickly.

"It turned out to be perfect," Hoyer said. "Yeah, and the shot-and-the-beer thing was such a perfect introduction to him to the Cubs. It was a great window into what he was going be like, and in hindsight, it was the perfect aesthetic for a Joe Maddon press conference. I think one of Joe's great qualities is he's every man. He gets along with everybody. He's the guy that can be talking about wine with the CEO to talking to any fan because I think he's done every job along the way. And I think people really respect the fact that he could kind of grind his way up to the job. He was a *longtime* minor league instructor. He always mentions that and he has sort of undying respect for those guys because of his role. And I think it really shows through in a lot of things he does."

At some point when Maddon started speaking, Cubs brass may have realized their days of being the face of the franchise were over. From the moment he took over, Epstein was the rock star on the team, not any of his players. His lieutenants, like Hoyer, were right behind him, explaining a rebuilding process unseen before in a major market. Over those first few years before Maddon's arrival, Epstein and Hoyer repeated their plan so much even they got sick of hearing it. But they knew it was needed. And it was all they had to say. In Maddon they had a new voice who could articulate a vision where rebuilding turned into winning.

"Well, first off, I felt like once we started winning I could fade into the background a little bit," Epstein explained. "You know, when the major league team is struggling and you're rebuilding your organization, you have more of a responsibility to be present and accountable for you [media] guys and to articulate a narrative for the fans and try to bring people along with the organization that you built. There's a natural transition once a team starts being competitive where the manager becomes more of the daily face of the team, as it should be. The ultimate goal is to have players who are the sole focus, day in day out, and we knew we were getting close to that point anyway. But then, on top of that, I knew if Joe got here he would fill your notebooks on a daily basis in a way that was pleasing to you and pleasing to him and pleasing to our fans, and there would be no one better at doing that. That was an added benefit."

It began in that room, at about the moment Maddon casually—perhaps flippantly—declared the Cubs' goal for 2015 was to make the postseason. The team was right in the middle developing a winning atmosphere but was still seemingly far from thinking about the playoffs. Though a pretty good second half finish in 2014 gave hope to the future, no one knew if that future was now. That didn't stop Maddon from declaring it so.

"I'm going be talking playoffs next year," Maddon said that day. "I'll tell you that right now. I can't go to spring training and say anything else. You have to set your goals high, because if you don't set them high enough you might hit your mark, and that's not a good thing. We're going to talk World Series this year, and I'm going to believe it. It's in our future."

To be honest, Maddon really didn't know if his club was good enough and frankly he didn't care. He knew there was talent and he knew there was a burgeoning positive attitude within the organization. Where would the harm be by adding to that enthusiasm?

"Why not?" Maddon would ask later with a smile. "I figured you set that goal every year. If you don't make it no one is going to hold you to it, but if you do it's great. And it's great to say it anyway."

Perhaps the message which resonated most with observers that day was Maddon's stated goal to be the same guy he was in the much smaller market of Tampa Bay. Even though he enjoyed plenty of success there he was able to stay somewhat under the radar. The Rays just aren't the Cubs, no matter how many playoff appearances they made under Maddon. The dress ups, the gimmicks, the distractions from the pressure were even more important in Chicago in Maddon's mind, considering the task at hand. The Cubs were synonymous with losing; it was Maddon's job to change that narrative and bring a winner to a place where winning was always an arm's reach away—if not further. The Cubby Bear, of all places, is where it started but hardly where it would finish.

"This is a guy that knows his role in the organization," Hoyer said. "I don't think there's a lot of managers that can walk into that setting obviously just totally off the cuff and really grab everybody, and he did it right away. And I think that was the kind of moment you realize, *Alright, this is a different kind of manager, a different kind of organizational asset for us.*

"I remember him going back to the office and he spoke to the whole office and it was clear at that moment that this is a guy that can captivate a room."

For Maddon, it was second nature. Sit in a bar and talk baseball. How hard is that? He knew the significance, however, of the challenge he was undertaking. He preaches living in the present but even he understood the job he was taking was no ordinary baseball gig.

"How about this? I'm sitting at the table back there and there's one window I can see out of, and there's the Wrigley Field marquee with my name on it. That was crazy. It just hit me. It was fabulous. You have to give Theo and whomever credit because they understood me enough to do it there."

Epstein can't remember all of the details from that day but he knows they made the right decision on a manager and where to introduce him. It simply fit the guy he was hiring.

"Yeah, it was great," Epstein said. "It smelled like beer."

To top off the day, at the end of the press conference, as Maddon was getting up to leave, he grabbed the microphone, speaking to the assembled media. "Where's the bartender?" he said. "I got the drinks right now. One round is on me."

As he turned to leave, he grabbed the mic again.

"That's a shot and a beer. That's the Hazleton way."

14

Early Optimism

WHEN PITCHER JON LESTER FIRST SPOKE OF PLAYING FOR JOE Maddon after years of facing him while Lester was a member of the Boston Red Sox and Maddon managed the Tampa Bay Rays, he sounded like a walking cliché.

"His teams always played hard," Lester said in the spring of 2015. "They were always a tough out. You had to be ready when you played the Rays."

But Lester wasn't just spewing things reporters and fans wanted to hear. He seemed to know what many would learn about Maddon after he took the job with the Cubs: his style is a mix of optimism and readiness, but where he stands out the most is in how he delivers his message. After playing for him for two years, Lester was reminded of his early comments about his new manager.

"It just always seemed they [the Rays] were ready to go every game," Lester stated. "They never seemed tired, you know. And I think that's what we saw last year [2016] with our guys as far as how he handles days off and how he handles the batting practice being optional, basically just letting us be who we are. And he knows how to talk to us. It always comes back to that with managers. Are the players buying what he's selling? The Rays bought in, so did we."

That idea of letting players "be who they are" is a theme attached to Maddon as much as any other managerial trait.

It applies to himself as well. When he arrived in Chicago he quickly declared he wouldn't be changing any of his tactics just because he was moving from a small market to a big one. The only exception was social media.

"I needed to tweet more when I managed in Tampa Bay because we needed fans to come to the ballpark," Maddon quipped. "I don't need to do as much selling here."

Maddon had only to sell his new players on himself. At the same time, his new bosses learned something about his sales job. Remember that declaration of making the playoffs at his opening press conference? It turns out it *wasn't* one of his gimmicks. None of his public persona is a gimmick, in fact.

"I think the thing that stood out that first spring is just how quickly I realized that his whole act, quote unquote, was not an act at all, that it was just authentically who he was and that the conversations that we would have behind the scenes were just another version of the types of conversations he'd throw out there for public consumption," Theo Epstein said. "And that his mind was creative all the time and his perspective was unique all the time, and it wasn't something he just did for effect.

"There was something really endearing to it that you had to feel, you had to sort of sit up in your chair and really engage with him in order to reach his level and that helped uplift you and anyone around you that interacted with Joe. So it was nice to have that realization, that it was super genuine, and it was authentic, and it wasn't manufactured in the least. Which is nice because you never know, when someone presents something for the public or for different audiences, how much is the real deal. And I like when things are organic so that was really a nice discovery."

Maddon's first goal with his new team was establishing trust. Being in the moment, keeping things organic, being *authentic*, these were the tools he would use to accomplish the job. And in Maddon's mind there was one more thing he wanted his players to see out of him as quickly as possible.

"Be consistent," Maddon said. "Players have to see you, as the manager or the leader, to be consistent when you walk in the door. Because when something happens in the game, they'll look at you in that corner of that dugout. They need to see consistency from that corner. They can't see you react emotionally in a negative way and be up and down all the time because if you do, they will be. So, whenever it's a bad moment, if you're in a season, or spring training, or of course, in the playoffs, I tell myself before I walk in the door, 'Remain consistent. Be yourself. Make sure that players see the same guy walk in.'"

Would those words be put to the test in the 2016 World Series? Maddon will tell you he *was* being consistent with his pitching moves but that's up for some debate. One thing no one debates is Maddon *was* the same guy, emotionally, in those heated moments as he was in his first spring.

Another thing which impressed Cubs brass early on was Maddon's willingness to lead with a soft touch. He didn't come in and overhaul the organization. After all, he was working with an accomplished president and general manager who, in Maddon's words, did a lot of the "heavy lifting" before the manager had arrived on the scene. In their estimation, Maddon fit right in—and then added a whole other layer of leadership. It was exactly what the Cubs front office wanted.

"His continued empowerment of [strength coach] Tim Buss to run the morning [in spring training], which we thought might be in jeopardy through the transition, was big," Epstein said. "His slogans were important, his disarming nature, his goofiness, his emphasis on humor and deconstructing norms, and pointing out the absurdity in the daily routine and in the game itself—and in ourselves—really opened up players to just relax and have fun and be themselves. And to feel like they were contributing. They had to be loose, because you would be dragging people down if you were too wrapped up, too serious, too tight. So he did a great job at creating a vibe that helped define our season."

Asked if there was a moment where he thought he gained the team's trust, Maddon paused, but couldn't come up with one. It helped that he had a reputation. Here was an accomplished manager from Tampa Bay, of all places. He had been to the World Series with an upstart, not a traditional power. It made a difference with players who bought in, if not for his resume then if for nothing else, his less-is-more approach. In Maddon's mind, he had already proven, for example, taking daily batting practice accomplished little—and possibly had a negative effect. Here was a baseball manager proposing a lighter work day. What player wouldn't buy in?

"If we don't feel like taking batting practice, we don't take batting practice," Lester said. "If you don't want to go out and throw, you don't have to throw. It's very, 'I know you guys are men. You know what you need to do to get ready to play every day so just go do it. I'll stay out of the way.' You don't have that leash on you all the time. You don't have to come out exactly at the time to stretch and stuff like that. There's a time and a place for that and we have structure but the structure is loose.

"I came from Boston where everything is, 'This is this, this is that, you do this, you take batting practice every day.' And it's like that in most places so this was a breath of fresh air to come over to this side and see this."

The Cubs admit the kind of structure Lester is talking about, and Maddon created, can only work if the team has the right set of players. One bad apple can wreck it all. Ben Zobrist admits there were a "few more closed-door meetings" with players when he and Maddon were with the Rays but Epstein and Hoyer had assembled a group who needed little scolding. It played right into Maddon's style and reinforced his optimistic nature. He saw the talent from afar, but when he began working with it he understood the group was special.

"It's the same philosophy I have with guys who are hot," Maddon explained. "People ask, 'What did you say to him?' I say, 'Nothing.' I want to stay as far away as I can when a guy is going good. The only thing we can do is mess that up. This team was full of young, self-motivated players. Do you think I have to say anything to Kris Bryant while he's hitting [nine] spring training home runs?"

The ease of his transition combined with the talent on the Cubs—as young and as raw as it was—led to Maddon being even more optimistic than usual. Again, it was no act.

"Joe was a real early believer in this team," Hoyer recalled. "He said things publicly, but privately, we would go in [to his office] after a lot of games and he'd be like, 'We're good, we're good. I think that team over there is not better than us.' Even though they might have had a better record, he really felt like we could compete with anybody. And early in the year, I was like, 'Okay, this is his style. He just says that.' And then as I realized, I was like, 'No, I think he really saw that we were just as talented, if not more talented than those other teams.' And I think his confidence really resonated with the group. I think the group knew that he believed in them. I think they saw that he wasn't just saying it, that he actually thought that we had a chance to compete in '15."

People often wonder how managers affect their teams outside of lineup and pitching decisions. Hoyer just relayed exactly how it happens. It's the vibe they create, the confidence they instill and the trust between manager and player that can make the difference. Hoyer admitted 2016 was a "different story." The team, by then, was a well-oiled machine. But early in 2015 is where the seeds were planted and the trust was earned. It was as if a first impression, at least for a manager, was the most important one.

"I've always given him a lot of credit for being one of the first people to realize that that team had a chance to compete when everyone just thought that [2015] was kind of a bridge year to 2016," Hoyer continued. "I think in 2015, it would have been really easy with the youth of that team to struggle a lot. We did for a little while but never where it buried us."

The transition to Maddon in early 2015 could not have gone smoother. He was building trust with his players and exhibiting the day-to-day communication skills which practically forced the Cubs front office to pursue him. They viewed letting him go work for another team as delinquent on their part, as if they were doing a disservice to the Cubs. So before even playing a regular season game, Maddon had convinced Epstein and Hoyer they had made the right call in hiring him. Not that they ever doubted it. This was a guy they liked being around as much as the next guy.

"You *do* want to be around him, you *do* want to talk to him. And so I think that's a big part of his success," Hoyer said. "He's so approachable and a person that relates to a lot of different people. I think when you're managing a clubhouse, with those disparate personalities, being a person that every one of those people likes to spend time with I think is really valuable. And it's probably something that you don't think a lot about in an interview process but ultimately, people gravitate towards him, and I think that's really a benefit. You can still win having a different personality but he happens to be charismatic and that adds a huge benefit."

There are real-time moments where the trust that spring made a difference. Lester relayed conversations with Maddon he may not have had with a less experienced manager. The left-hander was used to pitching deep into games having spent his entire career in the American League until 2015, but now there would be times he would have to be taken out for a pinch hitter. It didn't always sit well but the trust developed early on made the difference.

"There are documented and undocumented times where we haven't agreed on certain moves regarding being pulled or pinch hit for and I can go in there and vent to him as much as you want," Lester explained. "He'll listen calmly and give you the reasons why he did this or that. I figured that out early on that even if you don't agree with him you're going to get a good, calm, cool, collected, educated answer behind it. It may not be what you want to hear but he gives you that communication when you need it."

Maddon isn't the only manager to give those explanations, but in Lester's estimation he might be the most consistent.

"He's consistent about being consistent," Lester said smiling.

Those tough mound or office meetings don't occur without the foundation established in the spring of 2015. And the foundation isn't established without a plan from Maddon to earn the trust—though he came in with a highly touted reputation in the first place.

"He's got inherent credibility for having been a successful manager before," Epstein said. "He's not out to make anyone look bad. Joe doesn't demean anyone. There are a lot of people in positions of authority who like to reinforce their authority by demeaning other people, whether it's the players or their constituents or whoever's down on their luck. Joe doesn't do that, he lifts people up, so he's going to have players wanting him to be successful as much as he wants them to be. We saw that early in spring training and Joe kept that atmosphere throughout that first year."

15

Four Over Instead
of Four Under

ONE OF THE FIRST INDICATIONS THE CUBS HAD SOMETHING special in the dugout came after the first month of 2015. Until the regular season started, the only thing fans knew of Maddon, at least in Chicago, came via reputation and what they saw in spring training. But a team coming off 89 losses played better baseball in April than anyone could have predicted. By his own words, Maddon uses those first 30 days as a feeling-out process, especially after joining a new team.

"It takes about a month," Maddon said. "I don't know these guys. I don't know what makes them tick. And I don't know my bullpen. You can look at stats and talk to those who were here before but you don't really know until the season begins. It usually takes at least a month with a new team."

There were other reasons to expect little out of the Cubs early in 2015. For example, they had famously left Kris Bryant in the minors to start the season and still had holes on the team, both on their pitching staff and in the field. But before breaking spring training, Maddon had slowly pushed his team into a higher gear. In fact, in one of the few times as Cubs manager— perhaps the only time—he showed some annoyance in regards to how the team was performing during spring games. At the time the Cubs had taken Maddon's message of playing aggressive too far. "Never be afraid to make a mistake" was being tested, especially on the base paths, where the Cubs were running heedlessly during Cactus League games, perhaps in an effort to impress their new manager. After a while, he wasn't so impressed.

"We're not good at fundamentals in the game," Maddon stated at the time. "We have not done the little things right that permit you to win. The wins will happen if we get the fundamentals. The wins will never happen if you don't get the fundamentals."

Mind you, this was spring training, when rarely is a team judged by its play. Are the players healthy and are they getting their work in are usually the two issues at play. Maddon wasn't done setting a tone.

"It's guys being more concerned about survival as opposed to doing the right thing," he continued. "If we're going to change the culture here, they have to understand when you show up at the ballpark every day, it's not about survival. It's about winning.

"I'm a patient guy. I have to have even more patience knowing they're hearing another message again as a new manager. Not easy. We assume too much. When a guy gets to the big leagues we think because he's in the big leagues we don't have to cover [the fundamentals].

"The part that I cannot cope [with] standing in the dugout is when you're not a good fundamental team. That bothers me. And that can change. Experience or not."

It was a pretty intense moment for Maddon, as he's always been the pat-on-the-back more than a kick-in-the-butt type of coach. Ben Zobrist signed with the Cubs the next off-season so he wasn't around for the 2015 spring rant but he could only recall one other time Maddon had showed any emotion close to anger. It just wasn't his style.

"There's only been one time in all of my time with Joe that I've ever seen him blow up at the team," Zobrist said. "Once. That's how controlled he is. But there was one time after the All-Star break, when we were in Tampa Bay. And actually I believe you might need to ask Wade Davis about this. Wade Davis might have been pitching, starting that game. It was 2010, [I think], and we came out after the All-Star break, and we were totally flat. There was no energy, there was nothing happening, we were just sluggish. And he just went off. He came down the dugout and it was just, there were some curses in there. It was, 'Wake up!' There was a lot of just, 'We're playing the game again. You got to move on. We're not in the break anymore. Let's go, pick it up, pick it up!' And he usually doesn't have to do that, because players already.... There's already guys on the team that he sits down with you, like the leaders on the team in spring training."

Maddon recalled that moment with Tampa Bay in 2010, when the Rays began the second half sluggish.

"We were playing in Kansas City and we took a lead and everything, and we played a sloppy game and won.

"Everybody was real happy but me. I told [bench coach] Davey Martinez as soon as the game was over, 'Get them in the clubhouse right now. Get them in the clubhouse right now.' And I just, I had at them. I don't do that normally, but there was two things that occurred there I felt good about: we won, and it was on the road. If I'm going to get upset, I want to get upset after a win, not a loss.

"We were taking too much for granted. We didn't understand the gravity of the moment. We thought we could just show up and play and win."

In that particular case, Maddon had to take matters into his own hands but usually he'll rely on what Zobrist was referencing: Maddon's "Lead Bulls." Every spring he asks a group of veterans—and perhaps some younger players—into his office. The leaders of the team are given as much responsibility as possible in taking care of the clubhouse.

"Yeah, he'd sit down with the lead bulls and say, 'Hey, this is your team,'" Zobrist explained. "'I want you guys to police things. When you see something that shouldn't be happening, I want you guys to speak up about it. I want you guys to take ownership of this team.' And he's always believed in the player's responsibility, but that [in Tampa] was one moment where I remember he knew that he had to step up and say something because no one else was leading at the time."

Maddon felt the same was needed in spring training in 2015 and from that moment on the team played better. They *looked* ready for the regular season but that's really only viewing them in hindsight. There was too much in flux to really know if the Cubs could actually be good right away. First, there was the well-documented Bryant narrative. The Cubs weren't allowing the spring home run leader—and clearly one of the better hitters on the team—to break camp. If they did, they could lose him to free agency a year early. If they waited about 10 days into the regular season they would gain an extra full year of his services. The decision was easy for the front office and Maddon had to support it. It didn't mean Bryant's side had to like it.

"I don't want to say I'm mad or anything, I'm just extremely disappointed," Bryant said. "I wanted my performance to matter, and to me it felt like it didn't matter as much as I thought it would…. I'm definitely learning it's a business. I just go out there and put my head down and play as hard as I can. Baseball is such a performance-driven industry. I'm a big believer if you go out there and perform and work hard and you earn it then I believe you should get that chance to play up there. I guess it was viewed differently than I thought."

Though Bryant would be up soon enough, and wreaking havoc on opposing pitchers on his way to Rookie of the Year, it wasn't the most positive vibe around the team when it was announced he was going to the minors. Players always feel like the best 25 should be in the majors regardless of business and a few, like Anthony Rizzo, spoke their mind. So Mike Olt started at third base on Opening Day in 2015 while Tommy La Stella was at second. Everyone knew Bryant would soon be manning the hot corner in mid-April but no one could have predicted flashy middle infielder Addison Russell would soon follow. First off, Russell was a shortstop and he was only 21 years old. He was new to the Cubs, having come over in a mid-season trade with Oakland the year before. And he was playing behind multi-year All-Star Starlin Castro. Russell wasn't on anyone's radar in April 2015.

And then he was.

How Maddon handled Russell is a good look inside what makes him special. Bryant was the second pick in the draft, played three years of college, and was more than ready when he arrived at Wrigley Field. Russell would make it to the big leagues early, without college experience, and younger than Bryant. And now he had to learn a new position in a new organization as the Cubs moved him to second base. Russell struggled at times, but that's not the point. He survived. He and Bryant, along with other young players, were simply allowed to be themselves, warts and all. The atmosphere Maddon helped create was instrumental to their success and it came down to this: making mistakes did not mean being banished.

"It's just the way he puts things," Russell said. "When I first came up, he brought me into his office and pretty much just said, 'You're here for a reason; we believe in your talent, we believe in your ability. There's no reason to restrict that talent or ability, so go out there and have some fun. Don't be afraid to make mistakes.' Maybe it's what any manager would say. I don't know. But Joe, he put it in a way of, 'Make the aggressive mistake, have fun, smile. And at the end of the day, we're going to get better.'

"And the way that he put it was just...it just kind of hit home because the way that he explained it, it seemed more clear at the time. And just playing for him, you have this sense of individualism where you could go and do things that you want to do your way, but at the same time you get the job done. I think Joe doesn't [care] how it happens, as long as you get the job done. And then also the process of getting that job done for the next time as well. So I think that's really what I got out of that first meeting.… He has a lot of feel, as far as the players go, and he's just a great guy to explain things."

The result was a relaxed setting for young players to break in. And the Cubs were lucky with their veterans. They knew, in order to accomplish their goals, they needed their young talent to thrive. That part of rookie hazing where a young player can't be heard from was not part of the Cubs' culture. Epstein saw as much.

"If you take a step back, there's been this construct in baseball for a long time in which young players are to be seen and not heard and they have to subdue their personalities in order to prove that they belong and fit in," he explained. "And then, once the young player's established and a contributing member of the team, then they can show the world who they are. And that works great if you don't mind waiting two to three years for a young player to adjust and fit in, because that's how long it typically takes in baseball, if it goes well. We didn't have the luxury of that kind of time. We were relying so heavily on young players and we were going into our fourth year of the rebuild, we needed to start our competitive phase and so Joe [took] that norm and deconstructed it."

They were part of the group right away. It's a culture trait that exists to this day inside the Cubs' clubhouse. The sooner young players can be comfortable in their own skins, in a major league setting, the sooner they can thrive. Epstein saw the tone Maddon was setting very early on.

"I saw that first spring how he could create a vibe around a team, more so than specific interactions with players," Epstein said. "I think that's true of his method overall, that obviously he talks to players, but I've been around other managers who talk to players a lot more and interact a lot more, but I've never been around anyone who is so effective at creating a vibe that therefore ends up affecting all players, and just creates an environment that allows them to prosper."

Maddon probably isn't the only manager to create that vibe, but his ability to do so in a short amount of time—and with young players—is what stands out. He made sure Bryant's head was screwed on straight when he was sent to the minors and then pushed the right buttons with him and Russell when they came up in April. Even while newly signed free agent Jon Lester was having his problems adjusting to a new team and league, it didn't thwart the Cubs that first month under their new manager. It may not sound like much but being four games over .500 as May began opened eyes around baseball. Under normal circumstances the Cubs should have been about four games under .500. Was Maddon worth an eight-game swing?

"That first month I honestly didn't know what we were," Jed Hoyer said. "He did about as good a job as possible. How he handled those young guys coming up made a huge difference. That set us up for the rest of the year. Remember, Joe had made that declaration about the playoffs at his press conference. If we're buried in April we probably aren't thinking of the playoffs during that first half. But right away we were in the race. He did a great job."

A 12–8 record doesn't sound like much, but that first month would set the foundation for the Cubs to eventually fulfill Maddon's Cubby Bear promise. The playoffs were in their future.

16

Addison's Plight

THE ASCENSION OF SHORTSTOP ADDISON RUSSELL MIGHT BE the best illustration of how Joe Maddon handles young players. When he made his major league debut, on April 21, 2015, Russell was only 21 years old, with just 11 games played and 46 plate appearances at Triple-A. While everyone in baseball was awaiting the debut of 2013 first round pick Kris Bryant, Russell simply wasn't expected in the major leagues that soon—or even perhaps that year.

Unlike Bryant and 2014 and 2015 first round picks, Kyle Schwarber and Ian Happ, Russell had not attended college. He looked and played with less maturity partly because he was simply younger than the other players. The Cubs didn't even think his game was ready, but they called him up out of necessity to play second base. There was a lot on his plate, considering his age and his position switch. Russell was a career shortstop, drafted in the first round in 2012 by the Oakland Athletics. This is where Maddon stepped in, calling Russell into his office to tell his young charge to be who he is, have fun, and play his game. It was a pure Maddon message: make the aggressive mistake, have fun, smile.

This would be a theme that would come up over and over again with young players under Maddon. He figured out early as a coach and manager that talented players simply don't lose their talent when they get to the big leagues but that some guys don't make it because they aren't themselves all of a sudden. Mentally, they become something else, something other than what made them great.

"At the major league level, sometimes you kind of assume, *Alright, a guy is who he is*," Ben Zobrist explained. "He's going to either figure it out or not. It's up to him. But it's important for Maddon, it seemed, even from when I was young and it was his first year in Tampa Bay, that he wanted to create an environment that fostered that growth as a player, and I was in the perfect timing to experience that, and kind of be a part of that growth. He was just so encouraging to young players."

Zobrist played for Maddon as a young player coming up with Tampa Bay and, again, as a veteran with the Cubs. He says that positive nature about him hasn't changed. In other words he hasn't gotten bitter or less patient with age. In fact, he might be more patient now.

"To get where we want to go we need these young players," Maddon said. "It was the same in Tampa Bay. Why slow their progress by putting negative thoughts in their heads? The more mistakes they make the more they'll learn from them. And you know what? They'll make them again. But eventually the light will go on."

Past experiences shape who anyone is and that's no different for Maddon. He's been around positive- and negative-minded coaches and chose the positive path. But it goes further back than just baseball. His experiences in the game only fortified who he already was.

"I think I was really naïve growing up," Maddon said. "If there was one word to describe me it was 'naïve.' Through high school, through college, even [the] beginning part of pro ball, guys could mess with me a little bit because I just didn't quite get it all.

"Listen, I was part of the group and I had a lot of fun and all that but where I grew up and how I grew up kept me behind just a little bit. My dad passed away when I was 48, for as long as I knew my dad, he worked every day, never took a vacation, got up in the morning, put his work clothes on, and worked all day as a plumber. Then came back, my mom would have dinner ready. I can't tell you, maybe on one hand, I might remember him having four or five bad days in my life. So yeah, he was always positive about everything. That rubbed off. I'm going to be negative with a young player? What good would that do?"

It's in this environment that Bryant and Russell were brought to the majors in 2015. Bryant would probably excel no matter who his manager was because he had that kind of talent and mental toughness, but that can't be said of most young players.

Maddon's first big move with Russell was to bat him ninth while hitting the pitcher eighth. It allowed him to hide a little bit hitting low in the batting order but not be affected by the pitcher hitting *after* him. With a dynamic Cubs lineup coming into it's own, the last thing an opposing pitcher wanted was to nibble around a rookie and then have to face the top of the Cubs order. Russell would get pitches to hit without the pressure of hitting high in the lineup. It was brilliant.

"I can't deny hitting ninth took some pressure off me," Russell said.

Russell didn't light the world on fire right away but he was able to ease into being an everyday second baseman for a team on the rise. When April turned to May, Russell took off. He had a .806 OPS that month, and though that would be his best month that season, he quickly realized he belonged. He credits Maddon for making him comfortable so quickly.

There have been other moments, behind the scenes, when Maddon has excelled at communicating. During the 2016 season, infielder Tommy La Stella was having some doubts about continuing to play baseball. Instead of reporting to Triple-A when he was sent down to the minors, he went home to New Jersey. Maddon was a steady voice as he worked through the issue, but that foundation had been set a year earlier, at the end of the 2015 season.

"I said, 'Hey, at some point during the off-season can I talk to you?'" La Stella recalled. "'Just pick your brain on stuff.' Of course, he said yes. That conversation was the impetus towards shifting my approach towards everything. Baseball, myself, other people."

Maddon has often said trust is essential for a baseball team. Trust between manager and player, pitcher and catcher, front office and manager. It's the same in all team sports. The trust built up with La Stella a year earlier helped when the 26-year-old was contemplating retirement. Maddon was a guiding voice for him.

"I never would have expected anything else," La Stella stated. "There was no worry in my mind Joe would go in opposition. He kept in touch and was there for me. He didn't try to influence me or anything .He was just supportive. That's the best way I can describe him.

"As important as he is and his job is he finds a way to be egoless. He's not above joking around or being self-deprecating. That helps in those serious moments."

Another moment came in 2016, again involving Russell. He had just been voted by fans to start his first All-Star Game along with three other Cubs infielders. It was a historic moment he would share with first baseman Anthony Rizzo, second baseman Ben Zobrist, and third baseman Kris Bryant, except Russell wasn't enjoying it as much as you might think. Social media skewered the voting process, focusing their ire on Russell and his .237 batting average. Others were more deserving, in a lot of people's estimation.

Forget that Russell had nothing to do with the voting process; they took it out on him. And so did the baseball media. The day before the game, as Russell and his teammates were answering questions about making the team together, the shortstop was peppered with "Why are you here?" type inquiries. A wide-eyed Russell didn't know how to answer them. One of the greatest moments of his baseball life was being stepped on because some saw flaws in the voting process. In stepped Maddon.

"He asked me, he's like, 'Is this getting your attention off the field, or anything like that?'" Russell recalled. "I'm like, 'You know people have been talking, saying that I don't deserve this, I don't deserve that.' I mean, I felt great going into the All-Star Game, but yeah, I got those questions. And Joe was great. He told me not to worry about any it. He said playing with all these guys would boost my confidence, just being there.

"And I knew if I could just talk to a few guys, see these guys in a different atmosphere that I'm not used to, and then actually compete with these guys, after the All-Star Game, I believe that my confidence will be up. So I went to the game and had a great time with my family, played the All-Star Game, and then after that my confidence did kind of, just like Joe said."

Though his batting average didn't climb much, Russell had a very nice second half in 2016, proving—perhaps in hindsight for a lot of people—that he belonged in that All-Star Game. Again, Maddon's touch had an effect on Russell just as it did when he came up early in 2015. But Maddon's best work with the young infielder came later in his first year, long before he would make his first All-Star team. It would prove incredibly important for the Cubs as well.

The Cubs manager needed all of his master qualities as a communicator during the second half of 2015 if he was going to pull off something no one expected he would attempt mid-season. Not even his bosses.

"I think one of his best moments was moving Addison Russell to shortstop in mid-2015, that's what stands out," Theo Epstein said.

Benching an All-Star, then asking him to switch positions in favor of a rookie, needed to be done with tact. It was Maddon alone that decided, in August, Russell had to play shortstop in place of veteran Starlin Castro. And it was Maddon who broke the news to Castro, who had been struggling on offense and defense for much of the season. Still, it was a bold decision, made in the middle of the pennant race.

"Just that he would have the courage of his convictions," Epstein continued. "A lot of mangers would get wrapped up in this notion that, 'You can't do that to a veteran and that'll look really bad; I might lose veteran players if we do that.' And Joe just saw the essence of the baseball situation, that Addison Russell's really good at making the routine play, and some spectacular plays, and that's what we needed right at that moment at shortstop.

"And also he was great at seeing the essence of the personalities and that it would work, and that Russell was steady and mature enough and would earn the respect of the veterans, and that Castro—there was a way we could do it without losing Castro. He stayed connected to Starlin and made him feel good about himself; we ended up getting a great contribution out of him. So I just can't think of too many other managers who would've handled that entire episode from start to finish, from pounding the table to put Russell at short, to seeing it through with Castro, to resuscitate him for the playoffs and get a contribution from him the way Joe did. I thought that was incredible."

Russell was back at his natural position while Castro took off at second base, after a couple days on the bench. This came during an important confidence-building series with the world champion San Francisco Giants. The Cubs were still on the rise, figuring out who they were. They became something new, something better, with Russell at shortstop. They swept the Giants going 19–9 in August. Without getting through to Castro, it's possible things don't go as smooth. It could have been a big distraction.

"I did not give him any promises on how he is going to be utilized, other than, 'Just stay ready off the bench,'" Maddon said at the time. "I didn't want to give him any kind of false promises whatsoever."

Castro wasn't thrilled. To this day, his agent, Paul Kinzer, recalls him being unhappy, but Castro always appreciated Maddon's direct approach.

"Maddon was fine," Kinzer said. "It was tough for Starlin to move from the position he loved but Joe was straightforward about it. That's all you can ask for."

The Cubs were even more impressed Maddon didn't try to sugarcoat Castro's benching and subsequent position change. Stringing him along in any capacity would have turned the popular Cub against his manager. Instead, he picked himself off the floor and accepted his fate, which says as much about Castro as it does about how Maddon handled him. A team-first approach emerged.

"I think I can be good again," Castro said. "I think I can play.... We don't think about me, we think about us. It's the team now."

Castro hit .296 in August and .369 in September, playing a solid second base while Russell excelled at shortstop. The team took off as well. The move led to a second half run to the post-season, the Cubs first appearance there since 2008.

"He was a catalyst for that," Epstein said. "For me, it was something that we would do it the next year, we'd trade Starlin that winter and just do it the next year. But, he really felt from spring training on that our best team probably had Russell at short, which we all kind of agreed with. But that he felt at that moment it was important to do it, was a bold move. That was all Joe.

"It was that time of year, no doubt about it. The position that we're in, the manager has to have the unfettered ability to put the team on the field every single game, every single inning, that he thinks puts the club in the best position to win."

Russell never felt it was awkward with his teammate and he appreciated the faith Maddon showed in him. The same faith he showed at the very beginning of the season, when Russell was first called up, and before the All-Star Game in 2016. How he handled a veteran and a rookie proved telling in his ability to communicate—and it was his best moment as Cubs manager.

"I love playing shortstop and Joe allowed that to happen," Russell said. "That's when having a relationship with the manager helps. You're able to create that relationship with small conversations and then they build up to bigger conversations. And I think that's where Joe and I were and are. I feel there's a lot of trust there with all his players. There's a lot of faith. And as players that won a World Series under him we definitely support him for the type of mind that he has."

17

Embrace
the Slogan

AS IN ANY LEADERSHIP POSITION, GOOD COMMUNICATION IS essential to the success of a baseball manager. It's about being able to deliver a message and there may not be many in baseball more adept at messaging than Joe Maddon. There's one-on-one communication with players, which takes place behind closed doors, then there's the message for public consumption. And if Maddon learned anything while instilling his 9=8 slogan for the 2008 Tampa Bay Rays, it was that the length of the message doesn't necessarily increase its effect. In fact, less might be more, which dovetails his on-the-field philosophy as well.

When he took the job with the Cubs, Maddon insisted he would not change his style just because he was moving from a small market to a big one. His gimmicks, which played well in Tampa Bay, would still be a part of who he was in Chicago and that included his slogans. But he insists most of what he comes up with happens extemporaneously. Yes, the 9=8 campaign was inspired by some motivational tactics used by the Miami Heat, but it came to him on a bike ride, not during some brainstorming session with Rays brass. Likewise, his best sayings with the Cubs have come in the moment, not planned out.

"I think simplicity has a lot to do with it," Maddon explains. "I think the idea of going out and inundating these players with so much to think about, especially young players, is a mistake. It is honestly natural, they're not preconceived."

You wouldn't think of people in baseball being overly concerned with vocabulary—especially managers whose groans and grunts sometimes have to be interpreted. But Maddon is different. Though they come from different worlds, the Yale-educated Theo Epstein sees words as an asset to Maddon, perhaps unlike few coaches and managers he's been around.

"I think in his case, his use of language is the reflection of a creative mind," Epstein said. "I think he's got a lot of untraditional and iconoclastic thoughts, and so to properly express himself he's going to cast a wide net and grab on to certain words and phrases that resonate with him."

Whether he's devising a slogan for the season or speaking to the media several times throughout a day, Maddon has found words are his friend. Again, that's not typical for a baseball manager. Usually, the fewer spoken to the public, the better, as there's less chance for those words to be manipulated. Maddon doesn't see it that way.

"I've done a lot of reading," he said. "I used to read a novel every two weeks, for years. I've read Nelson DeMille, all of his stuff, Ken Fuller, much of his stuff, James Michener, Pat Conroy, all of his stuff as well. I like more of the contemporary guys. I really never got into the classics: Hemingway, Faulkner, Fitzgerald. I've never read those dudes; I like the present stuff. But anytime I read a book I'd always have a dictionary with me just because words are important."

Maddon had uncles who were "wordsmiths" and while coaching with the Angles he lived with another uncle who was a Harvard-educated doctor and a "brilliant man."

"He would challenge my vocabulary," Maddon recalled. "Every night I'd come back from an Angels game he'd bust my balls, man, I loved it. So Uncle Rick probably put the finishing touches on a lot of this stuff.

"Sometimes I'll actually not use a word, because sometimes I think people think, *He's trying to look smart*, so I'll dumb it down a little bit on purpose. Because sometimes you try to address your audience too. I never want to come off as being that guy that's trying to impress you with my mind. I don't and I'm not, it's just how I speak. Again it comes from reading and that's why I encourage reading."

It's with this background that Maddon tackles the big and small messaging needed to be a big league manager, especially in a market like Chicago. A lot of the time his messaging starts in the media. After all, he speaks with reporters more often than he does his team, at least as an entire group. He knows what he says to reporters will filter down to his players, who might only see a quick soundbite on television. That's where shorter is better.

"Respect 90," "Do Simple Better," and the "Process is Fearless" are a few examples of Maddon-isms which have taken hold over the years. But two in particular became hits in Chicago. When infielder Javier Baez came up from the minors in 2015, Maddon met with him as he would any new player to the 25-man roster. Having seen him play in spring training, and Puerto Rico the winter before, Maddon was extremely impressed with what the then-22-year-old could do on a baseball field. Though he had this extensive vocabulary to draw from, Maddon wasn't about to dig too deep with his rookie.

"I remember him sitting there in that little office in the old clubhouse," Maddon told Comcast SportsNet at the time.

"And he's sitting there right across the desk there and [I'm] just trying to loosen him up a little bit. I knew about his past—I got to know him; I went to see him down in Puerto Rico a couple years ago—and I just wanted to try and relax him a little bit…. That's what that's all about. We all, as professionals, one of the main things you do on a daily basis is try not to embarrass yourself. So how do you do that? By trying not to suck."

"Try Not to Suck" instantly took off. It spread across social media and quickly landed on a t-shirt, just as many of Maddon's other phrases have. This well-read man in his sixties had come up with a phrase schoolchildren might use on the playground. He hadn't planned to tell Baez that when he met with him, it just came out. As did another of Maddon's famous lines, which would become the rallying cry at the start of 2016.

"I thought 'Embrace the Target' was—of all the things that he's done—I thought that was the single best thing because it was true that despite the way that 2015 ended [losing in the NLCS], there was no question that going into 2016 we were going be the team that everyone was hyping," GM Jed Hoyer said. "I mean monster-hyped. I think it would've been really easy to try to downplay it. And he realized that was a futile attempt and embraced it, 'We're really good and people are going to want to knock us off and people are going to hype us.' Understand that's what's going to happen here…. It was really organic. He said it in a press conference or something."

In fact, Maddon had uttered those words during the winter meetings in December and then settled on them as his rallying cry in spring training. The Cubs were the clear-cut favorite to win the World Series and instead of downplaying it, the manager accepted it—without protest.

"I'm really a big believer in running towards the fire instead of away from it," Maddon said. "I wanted our guys to get comfortable with the concept of everyone speaking so glowingly of us."

Again, it wasn't a PR-tested phrase nor a meeting with Cubs personnel which led to the slogan. In fact, reading came in to play again for Maddon. Tom Clancy's *Clear and Present Danger* provided the backdrop for Maddon's new saying. In it, CIA agent Jack Ryan advises the president of the United States not to disassociate himself from a friend who had been killed during a drug bust.

"Jack Ryan pops up and says, 'No, Mr. President, don't do that,'" Maddon explained. "'Not only was he your friend, he was your best friend.' And he ran right into it and disarmed the entire moment. So it's my Jack Ryan moment."

It was brilliant. It actually took the pressure *off* the Cubs, at least a little bit. It's as if they were saying 'Yeah, so, what's your point?' when they were asked about being the favorites.

"I think he realized at that moment, we just need to embrace the fact that we're a team that people are going to talk about," Hoyer continued. "And I think he recognized we had a group of players you could say that to. I think he had thought we were a tough-minded group, guys weren't going to be scared off and he didn't need to coddle that group. He definitely thought they could handle the pressure instead of trying to deflect it like most people would do."

Hoyer and Epstein would see the culmination of a spring of embracing the target in 2016 when they flew out to Anaheim to join the team for Opening Night on April 4. They had been away from the team for those final days of spring training but rejoined them to open the season. The team had been inundated with an unprecedented amount of press for nearly two months. A day did not go by where Maddon and/or his players weren't asked about breaking their long championship drought and how this was "the best Cubs team" in years to do so. Knowing this, Hoyer and Epstein walked into the clubhouse and got a fresh sense of what was to come.

"We both walked in the clubhouse and we had the exact same reaction," Hoyer recalled. "Before the first game of the season even started, we were like, 'Wow, these guys are so focused right now.' It was a different energy I had felt before Opening Day, it was a totally different vibe. And I think the way Joe handled those expectations in the spring had a big part of it. That's why I think 'Embrace the Target' was one of his more brilliant moves."

Pitcher Jon Lester added, "It definitely worked. Maybe we win anyway, but everyone knew what was at stake. Everyone knew we were good. I never like to run away from any challenge like that."

In some ways, Maddon downplays that message as it just seemed like "the right thing to do." And like most of his messaging it was easy to swallow.

I don't over-inundate them with a lot of different stuff," Maddon said. "We are simple. We're very simple and we're very basic. They know my concept is that you're ready and healthy by the time the season opens. And of course, we're good. I mean we've got good players. A lot, though, are really young, so you have to take some pressure off whenever and wherever you can. I mean, they have enough at that age just trying to stay in the league, so I figured if we embrace it all it might do everyone some good."

Though new slogans and messages would pop up throughout the year, none encapsulated the team more in 2016 then "Embrace the Target." As bad as the Cubs were over the years, there were some times when they were the favorites, and it had always ended poorly. This time would be different, in some small part, because of three words. Sometimes, in messaging, that's all it takes.

"Why give big speeches if you can get your point across quickly?" Maddon opined. "And no one falls asleep that way."

18

A Fast Start

IN LEADERSHIP POSITIONS, KNOWING WHEN TO BACK OFF MIGHT be as important as knowing when to assert yourself. In fact, it may be more important because "doing nothing" isn't a concept people in management usually embrace, especially in baseball where there's always room for improvement. Though Maddon is known to be proactive with in-game moves—just ask his starting pitchers about being pulled—he also realizes when less-is-more applies to himself. In other words, sometimes it's good to get out of the way and let players simply play.

Maddon took that philosophy at the beginning of the 2016 season when his team began 25–6, picking up where they left off the previous regular season. Yes, they got swept in the NLCS by the New York Mets in 2015 but nearly everyone in baseball understood the Cubs went about as far as they could with their upstart team. They had maxed out on their season, but now it was time to raise the bar. Embracing the target didn't mean the goal was another Wild Card berth; the Cubs set their sights on much, much more. And Maddon sensed this in his team all spring as they worked towards that fast start.

"I don't view it as a new season," Kris Bryant said of 2016. "We're just picking up where we left off with a three or four month break in between."

Bryant could not have been more on point as he, himself, would adhere to those words following up his Rookie of the

Year season in 2015 with an MVP year the next one. He literally *did* pick up where he left off—as did the entire Cubs team. If Bryant sensed the mood then Maddon surely did as well. The Cubs knew they had unfinished business.

The hot start to 2016—despite a season-ending knee injury to left-fielder Kyle Schwarber—morphed into a runaway regular season, despite some tougher moments to come before the All-Star break. Some of those rough moments came when he had to pull his starting pitcher, sometimes simply to save him for the seventh month of the season. He joked that his job was to stand at the top steps of the dugout—as he does all game every game—and be a spectator like everyone else. Win or lose he was the same guy because he knew it was best for his team. They were still young but the lessons of 2015 were taking hold. It's the one attribute Jed Hoyer likes best about Maddon.

"I think his best quality is that he's the same person every single day," Hoyer said. "When I go in his office, I know exactly what to expect, and if I feel that way, then I think every player feels that way. And it seems like such an easy thing, but in this game you win 60 percent of the time, you're great. So most, almost half the time, you're walking into a guy's office after a loss and everybody knows losses probably feel worse than the wins feel good and he's remarkably consistent, day in, day out.

"I also think one of his great qualities is he's simply a great person to be around. That means players like to walk in his office and talk to him, that means coaches like to talk to him, that means a front office member, whether it's a win or a loss, like sitting down with him and chatting after a game. It's always really enjoyable. That's a great quality. When you see him, when you see him every day, being the same guy it helps whether you're winning or losing."

In this case it applied to the Cubs great start to the season. "Being the same guy" is usually associated in a good way with a losing team. In other words, the manager hasn't lost his mind despite his team struggling. Why can't that concept apply to a winning team as well? Of course, it's probably easier to keep status quo when a team is doing well but not every leader sees it that way.

"Shut up and get out of their way," Maddon laughed.

As the Cubs began a journey which would end in historic glory, Maddon kept the same face during losing and winning times. When asked often about being on pace to break the all-time major league record of 116 wins he seemingly answered it the same way he would have if they were on pace to lose the most games. It was always about the next day, not a grander picture.

Maddon sensed the same thing Hoyer and Theo Epstein did when they walked into the clubhouse in Anaheim on Opening Night. His team was ready and the last thing he wanted to do was get in its way. There would be times in 2016 he would have to manage but during the team's 25–6 start most of what he had to do was find enough playing time for his talented roster. Otherwise, he watched as a juggernaut took hold on their march to a division title. What began in 2015 carried over to 2016 with the Cubs manager simply letting it play out in front of his eyes.

"I sensed they were ready to start the season," Maddon said months later. "Obviously, they were. Staying out of their way was the best thing for them."

That steady hand would be needed in time when the Cubs would face their first losing month under Maddon.

19

The Hiccup

THE BEGINNING OF THE 2016 SEASON COULD NOT HAVE gone better for Joe Maddon's team. After breaking away from the pack with a 25–6 start, the Cubs settled into their place atop the baseball world, seemingly without any worries. On June 19 they had won their third consecutive game, this one 10–5 over the Pittsburgh Pirates, which pushed their record to 47–20. Their lead in the division grew to 12.5 games that day partly because the other four teams in the division were on a combined 15-game losing streak. Their closest two competitors, the St. Louis Cardinals and Pirates, each were nursing five-game losing streaks of their own. The Cubs seemingly had the division locked up well before Independence Day, an unheard-of achievement.

But then things changed, and for the first time since the NLCS loss to the New York Mets the season before, Joe Maddon had to face adversity. A less-experienced manager may have viewed the next three weeks differently. A 6–15 record halted the Cubs runaway season in its tracks.

Team brass wasn't leaving anything to chance in attempting to figure out what was going wrong.

"Theo and Joe and I had a lot of meetings during that period and I think we all knew that there was going to be moments during the course of the season that it's not going be a magic-carpet ride, that's just not how this works," GM Jed Hoyer said. "But to Joe's credit, he was much calmer than Theo or I were about it. We weren't panicked but we were definitely concerned about just fettering away that lead."

That lead would eventually shrink to seven games, a much more manageable number for the opposition. Both the Cardinals and Pirates suddenly were within striking distance at the All-Star break. For anyone associated with the team—especially Maddon—the root of the problem became evident over the course of those three weeks.

Fatigue.

On June 17, the Cubs began a stretch of 24 games played in 24 days. It may not sound like much to the average person, but there is a reason the league has to get approval from teams to play more than 20 consecutive days. It's unusually taxing.

Because of a makeup game against the Atlanta Braves on July 7, the Cubs would play every day right up until the All-Star break. It killed them and the baseball world wondered if the "cursed" Cubs had returned. Maddon insisted things would change after a break.

"We were gassed," he said. "Anyone could see it."

Certainly anyone associated with the team saw it, but that didn't mean a lot of man hours weren't used in trying to change their fortunes—though little could seemingly be done about it in the end. For whatever reason, it affected the starting staff the most. Perhaps they needed that built-in extra day a team gets every seven to 14 days. With no break, they wilted.

"We were just concerned, because we were so flat, so bad for so long, and that we were looking for the reasons why, and talking to our players, and every player kept saying, 'I just think we need to get to the break; I just think we need to get some rest,'" Epstein recalled. "And when your job is to figure out what's happening, and why, and then help make it better, that's not a real satisfying answer."

In other words, what can a front office—or manager—do if the answer is rest? They can't materialize an off-day out of thin air nor could they start skipping starters because the Cubs were short on depth in that area anyway. Maddon was already rotating position players in and out, but nothing stopped the skid. This is where the manager showed his consistency in the dugout. He didn't rant and rave or close ranks, he stayed the course.

"It's easy to have meetings when we're losing and panic and all that," pitcher Jon Lester stated. "[Maddon] knew the stretch we were going through was part of the game and part of baseball. He knew it would change. And besides, what could he do? The schedule had us playing every day."

The low point may have occurred in New York, where the Cubs had swept the Mets the season before. But the Mets had gotten their revenge in the playoffs with a sweep of their own, so now came the so-called rubber match. A four-game series with "rematch" headlines attached to it.

The Cubs barely showed up, losing all four games by a combined score of 32 to 11. The lowest of the low points came in the finale on Sunday when Lester lasted 1.1 innings, giving up eight runs, the day before the July 4 holiday. The Cubs' lead was single digits by then, just eight games.

"Joe does a great job of staying out of the way," Lester said, shaking his head as he recalled that day. "There was no panic. He just kept running us out there knowing a change would come, either soon or after the All-Star break. He didn't waver in the belief that we were just gassed."

Maddon wasn't as concerned about losing games as he was about the mental state of his team. *He* was confident they would turn things around but what if doubts started to creep into the heads of his players. Things could get worse.

"I knew we would turn it around," Maddon recalled. "It's just a matter of staying with the process. You have to make sure that the guys know that too."

The team's mental state—and Maddon's fortitude—continued to be tested in early July, before the All-Star break, as the lead continued to shrink. A series loss to the Reds, after the debacle in New York, was followed by the makeup game which contributed to their downward spiral. A night game at Wrigley Field on Thursday, July 7, and then a late-night trip to Pittsburgh had Maddon shaking his head.

"Why play a makeup night game and then fly?" he opined more than once. He'd have to ask the Cubs business office that question, because no one else knew the answer. The Cubs lost to the Braves that night then arrived in Pittsburgh at 5:30 in the morning for the final three games of the first half. The lead was still eight but the Pirates and Cardinals were showing signs of life and the doubters were out.

"When we were 25–6, the media was asking questions about, 'How do we balance getting our players rest with going for the all-time wins record?'" Epstein said at the time. "I attached zero meaning to that. I called bullshit on that question. The same way, if I think people are getting too down on us for not playing well, I'll call bullshit on that, too. I just think all that matters is how we respond to adversity and how we handle success."

Maddon kept on repeating the same thing so much, people grew weary, but what else could he do? This is what he believed and he isn't one to steer away from what he thinks is the truth just to change the narrative. The story in his mind was about overtaxed minds and bodies and nothing else.

"It's been a run without a break," he said while in Pittsburgh. "Fatigue enters in for everybody, if they want to admit it or not. It was a tough three weeks. It was a fatigue situation more than anything. When you're fatigued, you try to manufacture something that's not there."

It had been evident in how the Cubs were playing across the board. Pitching, hitting, and defense all succumbed to the schedule and Maddon was so sure of it he did nothing but wait until the All-Star break arrived. He would be proven right in every possible way in the second half, as the Cubs never again played that poorly in 2016. Perhaps other managers would have handled things just as well but it was hard for the front office to imagine someone doing any better than the guy they had in their dugout.

"Joe was remarkably calm because I think he felt like the All-Star break was this great circuit breaker for us to take a deep breath," Hoyer said. "And you look at it, I mean, we had a really tough series coming out of the break. We started with Texas, then we had the Mets, then we got [Aroldis] Chapman and then we just really took off after that.

"Like I said, I think Joe really saw it for what it was, which is a tired group. And maybe we did expend a lot of energy grabbing that lead and maybe that tired our guys out. Our starters had been going on turn really consistently. I think that was one regret that we had, is we probably should've gone to a sixth man earlier just to kind of break it up. But no, Joe was really calm in those moments. Didn't ignore the fact that we were losing the games, but certainly didn't overreact to that fact, and I think the players respect that."

Lester added, "I think there's a time and a place for meetings and rah-rah and all that stuff and this wasn't it. Again, there was nothing that could be done but get to the break at that point."

The Cubs would lose the first two games in Pittsburgh, seeing their lead shrink to 6.5 games with the Pirates in the middle of a 9–1 stretch. The final day before the All-Star break would prove to be a big one. Rarely do teams put much stock in one game which isn't played in September or October, but in this case, a 6–5 win over the Pirates really did *feel* important.

"Winning that game before the break was rather large," Maddon admitted.

No one could really put a finger on why it was so big but a seesaw affair on that Sunday ended in the Cubs' favor after Kris Bryant singled home Matt Szczur with the go-ahead run in the eighth inning. A collective breath was had after the game.

"As much as there was a must-win game, it was today," Anthony Rizzo declared.

The lead was back up to seven games. That's as close as the competition would get for the rest of the season but no one could know it for sure at the time. No one but Maddon, at least.

"It's undeniable that we didn't play well for a long stretch of time," Epstein said. "Once you go through that as a club, then you know it's possible. You get to the edge of the abyss and you stare right in. You go, 'Hey, we're not going to just rack up the wins. You have to go out and earn it.' That can be a good thing for our team. Joe saw that."

Maddon did indeed believe it would be good as well. In moments much later in the year, the Cubs could call upon their lone adversity during the regular season and remind themselves how it felt. In this case, getting out of their rut simply consisted of getting some rest, though that didn't stop the questions from coming during the break. Seven Cubs participated in the Midsummer classic but instead of adoration for their first half accomplishments reporters pestered them with questions about "choking." Remember, their second-half resurgence was still days away from beginning and they had just gone 6–15.

"The only people panicking about this is the media," Rizzo said after the break. "No offense to you guys. It's been pretty negative, all the comments coming out of everyone's mouth except in this clubhouse. We feel great. We feel great to be back together and we're ready to go.

"It's July and you need stories to write about, and what better story to write about than why are the Cubs struggling? The only people worried about it are outsiders."

After the fact, people within the Cubs credited Maddon with instilling that kind of confidence in his players to speak up in such a way. After all, Rizzo could not have known what was to come while Maddon only had an idea, not a crystal ball. Unlike his first baseman, the Cubs manager never took any criticism to heart. In fact, he turned it around.

"The noise coming from outside is necessary," Maddon said. "It can serve as motivation and it's also just fans being fans. It's about how you channel all that."

How did Maddon channel the moment when the Cubs began to tank? He did nothing. Considering the criticism which was to come in the playoffs later in the year, how he handled the pre-All-Star-break collapse is especially noteworthy. He didn't over manage. He simply kept to a belief which would ring true—that his team was exhausted—which ironically led to some wasted energy by his bosses.

"It seems like a cliché answer," Epstein admitted about a team needing rest. "Joe was really adamant that he had his finger on the pulse of the club, and he agreed that we just needed to get to the break, and sure enough, we just needed to get to the break, and Jed and I wasted a lot of time and energy on it all."

After the All-Star break in 2016 the Cubs went 10–6 the rest of July and then 22–6 in August to blow away the competition. The division would be theirs by a huge margin, just as they had foreshadowed with their great start to the season. Their hiccup was over, thanks in part to their manager's quick understanding of the situation. Maddon didn't do a lot during the losing skid, because there was nothing more to be done than show support.

"I had gone through it before with the Rays," Maddon said. "We lost seven in a row before the All-Star break in 2008 when we went to the World Series. That was totally different. With the Cubs, we were gassed. Simple as that."

20

American Legion Month

AT LEAST ONE THING SEPARATES JOE MADDON FROM A LOT OF his colleagues, especially from so-called "old-school" skippers who frown upon days off for players. But times have changed—specifically game times—and Maddon has learned from past experiences. When it's time to push, he backs off. He's proactive in doling out rest just as he is in pulling his starting pitcher. And with travel more hectic than ever, and rotating start times, Maddon would rather err on the side of caution then the other way around.

He has a theory: Resting players more than the norm can allow for a second-half push just as other teams are feeling fatigue. August can be a brutal month, both in climate and in the grind. September has a momentum of its own, according to Maddon, as playoff teams can smell fall baseball approaching. But there's a reason they call August "the dog days," though the Cubs have avoided a drop off in part due to Maddon's philosophies. In his first two seasons as manger, the Cubs went a combined 41–15 in August, including a sizzling 22–6 in 2016. The nervousness the team brought upon its fan base before the All-Star break quickly faded as they dominated the competition. The Cubs don't believe that winning percentage over the last two years is a coincidence.

"Oh no, it's not a coincidence at all," GM Jed Hoyer said. "I remember when I was with the Red Sox, always feeling like the

Rays [when Maddon was manager] played great at the end of the season. Why is that? And I do think part of it is that there's an accumulation of moments over the course of the year where Joe discourages batting practice and tells guys to come in later. And people might think that only has value in that moment, but I think what Joe realizes is that there is a bank account to part of that. You're [making deposits] in an energy savings account and I think that our guys have been really fresh and healthy down the stretch."

Where did the idea of less-is-more originate for Maddon? From his days as a coach with Angels, before becoming a manager. He saw teams play their worst baseball at the most important time of the year.

"One of the things we did was hit a lot, and we'd hit on Sunday mornings for an hour," Maddon said. "In retrospect, I'd see guys fade by the end of the season. I was the hitting coach, and I was in the middle of all that. I thought that was the right way to do things, too."

But it wasn't the right way—though few, if any, in the game would think backing off when times are tough would be an answer. It's exactly the time to let up, according to Maddon.

"People think young players don't have to get rest," Maddon stated. "They need it more than older guys sometimes because they don't know how to pace themselves. You have to take a mental break in this game. I don't care what anyone says. I've seen it."

So as the Angels experienced some less-than-stellar finishes to their season, Maddon kept it in the back of his mind: rest is as important as work.

"I think he recognizes the marathon of this thing better than other people," Hoyer said.

When he became manager with the Devil Rays he began to implement his philosophies, but then took it to another level the year after Tampa Bay went to the World Series in 2008. He saw a fatigued team coming off a long postseason run and backed off even more.

"He figured out they needed a break," longtime bench coach Davey Martinez explained. "It's a grind every day. Guys need a break. So we told them to come later to the park. Show and go."

American Legion Week was created. It's really American Legion month because Maddon tends to back off during all of August, but for one week every year at this time he allows his players to simply show up and play.

"When I was young I would have a day job then go play American Legion ball," Maddon explained. "You would work until 5:00 PM then just show up and play. So that's where the name came from. We'd buy an American Legion banner and make a whole thing of it."

He kept up the practice after arriving in Chicago, believing it would help performance that month and in the final one as well. When he saw the Cubs wacky schedule, which combined a steady stream of day and night games, it only fortified his beliefs.

"This is the time of the year that you really have to fight through," he said. "I'm talking post-All-Star break into August, because this is the time when you're a little bit fatigued. That's why we're doing the American Legion Week. If you're able to maintain at this particular point, here comes September and I promise you our guys will be charged up every day. September provides its own energy."

Since implementing American Legion Week—which essentially lasts a month—Joe Maddon's teams went 130–91 in August through 2016. The Cubs took control of the Wild Card in 2015 and further cemented their status as the best team in baseball in 2016 during that month. Rotating players in and out of the lineup while allowing them to show up later paid off in a big way. Maddon was able to withdraw from that "bank account" of rest he built up as the two seasons were coming to their conclusions.

"It's not going to happen every year," Hoyer said. "But I do think that it's part of the way he manages, that he allows guys to not grind themselves down. And listen, why do they call it the dog days? Because the mental grind is really difficult, the physical grind is difficult, and if you could make that less of a grind, which Joe does, I think there's a great benefit.

"I think he's one of the few people that's willing to take that chance. Because if you don't take batting practice and you show up late and do all those things, you're not winning, it's easy to be a target. I think Joe believes, *I don't care about that. What I care about is I think this right.*

This is the essence of Maddon. Think about the alternative. Who would be critical of his teams if they took *more* batting practice or if he played his star players every day? Almost no one. It sets him up for criticism but he pays no attention to it.

"Just because something has been done for many years doesn't mean it's the right way of doing it," Maddon has said often.

Maddon challenged the norms of batting practice, of players playing 162 games, and of the macho notion that rest equals weakness. In the same way he figured out rookies need to be brought into the fold quickly to help him win he also realized to get the best out of them—as well as the veterans—he needed to alter other norms. Rest was a friend, not something to fight.

"I don't care what is says on their birth certificates, everyone needs a break in this game," he declared.

No one can argue with the results. That's not to say other methods don't work as well, but most of those don't address the ever-changing landscape of modern baseball, which involves arriving in cities at the wee hours of the morning more often than ever before. The Cubs might have the most upside-down schedule due to a restriction on night games. Do players love the strategy of sitting so much?

"I'm not going to name names but there are times I tell a guy he's getting a break and he's like 'What?'" Martinez said. "But no one complains they're being asked to come to work two hours after the rest of the league. He took a chance because we would be criticized if it didn't work, but it has."

The players ultimately have the final word if a strategy works or doesn't. Though none would ever go to their manager and ask for more time off, all appreciate it. And the results showed up in the standings. American Legion Week is a hit. Even the ultimate baseball rat sees the benefit.

"I love to take swings," former MVP Kris Bryant said. "But you need a break in this game. Joe gets that. He's always thinking of us. I've only had one manager, but he understands the physical as well as the mental part of the game. And then gives us some space."

A strong finish in 2016 combined with their strong start to the season led the Cubs back to the playoffs and eventually the World Series. American Legion month had no small part in it.

21

Games 6 and 7

ALL OF JOE MADDON'S EXPERIENCES AS A COACH AND MANAGER would be put to the test in Games 6 and 7 of the 2016 World Series against the Cleveland Indians. Little did he know at the time, but his decisions the next two days would have a profound effect on the outcome. And though he would be the man to lead the team known as the "Lovable Losers" to their first championship in 108 years, he would face an off-season of questions and criticisms about those moves.

The questions would all revolve around his pitching decisions, mostly as it concerned closer Aroldis Chapman. Chapman had thrown 42 pitches in Game 5, normally knocking him out of commission for several days, if not for this being the World Series. Chapman did have a day off between Games 5 and 6 and declared himself ready for whatever was to come. Maddon would lean on him again for the final two games, leading to a lot of raised eyebrows.

Though Game 7 would receive the most attention, it was Maddon's Game 6 decisions which created his dilemma that was to come. Leading 7–2 in Game 6, he brought Chapman into the game in the seventh inning. It was hardly a save situation and considering the closer's Game 5 workload, many were left wondering if it was the right move.

"It was the middle of their batting order," Maddon explained afterward. "There was just no other way to look at that and feel good, man. That could have been the ballgame right there. I thought the game could have been lost right there if we did not take care of it properly."

Chapman entered with two men on base, two outs, and the dangerous Francisco Lindor up. He induced a groundout from Lindor, ending Cleveland's threat, but not Chapman's night. Maddon would further explain he much preferred Chapman pitching with a cushion against the Indians' top hitters, than later, in potentially a closer game. If another reliever had messed up, Chapman would be called upon with much less margin for error with potentially less then elite stuff considering the recent workload. Maddon preferred Chapman with a little breathing room. There was some sound thinking in that decision perhaps based on something which occurred about eight years earlier.

In 2008, Maddon's Tampa Bay Rays team was playing the Boston Red Sox in the American League Championship Series, ironically led by Theo Epstein and Jed Hoyer. It was Thursday, October 16, 2008. The Rays got out to a 7–0 lead only to see Boston score eight runs in the final three innings to stun Maddon and his team with an 8–7 victory. Maddon didn't have a Chapman to turn to, but he knew the idea of holding on to a big lead in the playoffs wasn't as simple as hoping the other team doesn't rally. He wanted to be proactive.

"That was a really tough day," Maddon said in recalling that game. "It reminded me that nothing is over until that last out is made, especially in the postseason. It's definitely different than the regular season. There is no next game. I know people have a hard time when I remind them of that. If you blow the lead because you don't use [whoever] then you're heavily criticized for that. But it's not about being heavily criticized. It's about being proactive and seeing things before they happen."

So eight years later, Chapman got out of the seventh inning then went to the mound to pitch the eighth inning of Game 6 of the World Series with the score still 7–2. Maddon wasn't about to use up his best pitcher for one out, with two innings to go, no matter what the pitcher did two days earlier. Chapman set the Indians down in order in the eighth, using a total of 15 pitches between the two innings. The Cubs were one inning away from forcing a do-or-die Game 7.

When Anthony Rizzo homered in the top of the ninth inning, giving the Cubs a 9–2 lead, it felt like Maddon had made all the right moves. He used Chapman *before* the game got close, allowing his offense a chance to extend the lead. It worked. And now was the time to get Chapman out. Maddon knew it, his bosses knew it, millions watching around the world knew it. The Cubs had one more game to play and they might need their closer once last time. After 57 pitches over the course of the last two games—plus a seven-run lead—it was time.

Except it didn't happen.

There was no one ready in the bullpen. In fact, it wasn't until Ben Zobrist walked, after Rizzo hit his home run, that the bullpen got moving. Pedro Strop began to warm up in a hurry but the inning ended too quickly, after Addison Russell grounded out, meaning Chapman would have to start the ninth. He would eventually come out, in favor of Strop, but only after walking the leadoff hitter on five pitches, not including his warmups that inning. There was only one person to blame for the blunder.

"Yeah, it was all me," Maddon said. "I had it in my head. When I put Chappy [Chapman] in the game to begin with, first of all, it was against Lindor, and I thought there's no other way to do this because if they get back in it—I've had bad games in Cleveland before—we had to put him in there. I wanted Lindor right handed, etc. so we put him [Chapman] in the game there. And I also had told myself, actually before the game, is that if you get a big lead and you have to use him early, make sure you get somebody up and get him out. So I had it in my mind to do that and I just didn't say it to [pitching coach] Chris Bosio in time."

Would that decision come back to haunt Maddon the next night? After all, it was only five extra pitches and a few easy warmups. But combined with his stint on Wednesday, Chapman had thrown 62 pitches, way more than he had in any back-to-back outings all season.

"I feel blessed that I'm just healthy to pitch in this situation," Chapman said after Game 6. "This is [why] the Cubs brought me over."

It's the one move Maddon regretted. How could he forget to get a pitcher up?

"Because you're thinking about so many things offensively, and you get through the moment [the home run] you wanted to get through, and I'm thinking to myself, *If we score right here, you have to get him out.* So I'm thinking then, *Inning's over, inning's over.* And I'm waiting, waiting, I said, 'Get Stropy up.' And I just said it too late."

In the stands, the press box, and throughout baseball, Maddon understood the questions that would follow. Why was Chapman still in the game?

"It's funny because this is the honest truth, had that been a game, a different game, I probably would have gone down and been like, 'Hey, what happened there?'" GM Jed Hoyer said. "Right? But I don't know...Theo was very aware too, in the playoffs. I think it's really important that the managers and coaches are confident that we don't go down there and cause a storm in the World Series because these guys need to play the next day. We have one more day left and you're not worried about your process.

"Normally you'd be like, 'Okay, how do we fix this, because we have 100 more games left?' But in that situation, all you want is like, 'Let's not upset the apple cart and let's win the next game.'"

The Cubs would do that, but not without plenty of consternation the next night as well. Many would attribute Chapman's struggles in that game with the extra pitches he had thrown the previous day. It would be a narrative that made some sense and would certainly stick after Chapman's velocity took a nosedive in Game 7.

Game 7 played out a lot like Game 6, at least early on. The Cubs got out to a 5–1 lead heading into the bottom of the fifth inning, with Maddon keeping a close eye on Kyle Hendricks. Hendricks was doing well, allowing only a run on four hits until a two-out walk to Carlos Santana ended his night. The manager called on Jon Lester, setting off another round of questions, but Maddon had this all planned out. He wanted to get five innings out of Hendricks and then use Lester as a bridge to Chapman. But with Jason Kipnis facing Hendricks for a third time Maddon didn't want to take any chances. A 5–1 game could be 5–3, so he switched his pitcher and catcher as David Ross entered with Lester.

"We were all ready for Game 7," Lester explained. "We were ready for Game 6 too, if something weird happened. I actually texted Joe before Game 6. He said, 'No, unless something weird happens. If we win tonight then tomorrow, for sure.'

"Before the game he made things clear on what the plan was. As we all know plans in this game don't always go as planned. We had a heads up."

So Lester entered in a "dirty inning" (with a man on base) instead of starting the next one.

"I had Lester hot and didn't want to wait to bring him in if the inning got worse," Maddon said.

Things went as bad for Lester and Ross as could be imagined. A single, a throwing error by Ross, and a wild pitch plated two runs, reducing the Cubs lead to 5–3. Did it bother Lester to enter the game early?

"I had no problem with that move and we can all second guess things because it didn't go as planned, but we all knew what was going on," he stated. "I didn't have a problem. At that point I'm hot so if I'm going to get in this game let's go and try to execute.

"In that situation, anything flies. It's the last game of the year, you're figuring it out as you go. Anytime you run in from the bullpen in Game 7 your adrenaline will take care of anything you need."

Lester would settle down but some damage had been done. Hoyer says that moment is a reminder why baseball is such a game of inches. Hendricks was *that* close to getting out of the inning, which would have allowed Maddon to stick to his original plan.

"The one thing that's always bothered me: Did Hendricks have Santana struck out?" Hoyer asked. "Looked like the ball was in the entire zone. They punch him out right there…does everything change? Now all of a sudden he's through that inning because he was pitching so well. Joe might send him back out for the sixth [or Lester starts a clean inning]."

The Cubs didn't get that call, leading to two runs in the inning and now forcing a closer game than anyone wanted. But Maddon's plan was still intact. He had Lester pitching with a lead and Chapman ready to go when needed. The next decision would be another big one: When should he go to the closer coming off his 62 pitches over the course of Games 5 and 6?

"There are lots of different ways to attack it and what's most important is that the manager has thought through all the sides of it, all those scenarios, and makes an informed decision, weighing the variables that he sees as most important," Theo Epstein said. "He's not always going to be right and he's not expected to be. And he's not always going to err on the side of logic versus the human being, and he shouldn't. He should pick and choose what makes the most sense, and that's what he did. Obviously, not everyone, including his bosses, are going to agree with every decision he's supposed to make."

The Cubs would extend the lead to 6–3 on a Ross home run while Lester continued to pitch the sixth, seventh, and eighth innings. It was after a two-out single in the eighth that Maddon came to get Lester in favor of Chapman. He wanted Chapman to get four outs and, again, he didn't want him entering in a closer game. As with Hendricks, the question later became: Could Lester have finished the inning?

"There are always controversial moves," Lester said. "In any game, at any time. The way you look at it is, what was Chapman there to do? He was there to close Game 7 of the World Series."

But Chapman wasn't able to close it out. A double by Brandon Guyer after Lester was pulled followed by a home run to Rajai Davis changed everything. The game was tied 6–6. Those extra pitches by Chapman in Game 6 now became a bigger storyline.

"The unlikely guy to hit a home run, hit a home run on a 98 mile per hour fastball," Lester continued. "I don't care if he [Chapman's velocity] was down a little because he was used. He was there to win that game."

Somehow Chapman got through the ninth inning unscathed and then a short rain delay came. Maddon grabbed his dad's hat in his office while Jason Heyward gathered the team in the weight room. All was not lost, as the Cubs won the World Series with a two-run 10th inning. That didn't stop the critics from having a field day with Maddon.

"What I've said all along is that I think if you look back at Game 7, I think he managed the way Joe manages a lot of games; he does some unconventional things," Hoyer said. "Over two years, I think both Theo and I have recognized that he knows our team, he knows our personnel, he's willing to do things that other people aren't willing to do and it almost always works out.

"And I felt like he had a plan in Game 7, he wanted to use Lester in the middle innings, he wanted to get to Chapman and I think a lot of his moves in Game 7 didn't work out. I think the process was the same, the person making those decisions was the same. It's a game of probabilities and…whether it was Lester coming in right away [and] giving up those two runs or whether it was Chapman coming in, just those moves didn't work out in those moments."

The idea of pulling a pitcher *before* he gets into serious trouble has always been a staple of Maddon, perhaps going back to that 2008 ALCS Game 5 loss. It's why he sometimes has to have difficult conversations with starters who think they should remain in the game. How many times has a manager done the opposite, pulling a starter after it's too late? So Maddon was true to his convictions, but that doesn't mean he made the right calls.

"I think there's a time for focus on process and that's most of the time," Epstein said. "There's a time to focus on results and that's when you're talking about championships. And it's a *fact* that without Joe Maddon we don't even have the opportunity to get to a Game 7, we don't have the opportunity to get to a World Series, we don't have the opportunity to probably win a division, so that ends the argument right there.

"And then all the decisions are tough decisions, that are 55/45 [percent] one way or the other, and some come down on the side of the percentages and follow what makes the most pure, logical baseball sense and other times you want to come down on the side of the human beings involved, and sometimes you want to manage for that second and sometimes you want to manage for the length of the series or the season.

"Taken in its totality, he was a major catalyst in helping us win the World Series."

Lester adds, "Even if we lose that game, he's our manager, he's our guy. You stand behind him 100 percent, no matter what. You can pull anyone you want out of the stands—Do you think you could do better? It's easy from your couch, but in the heat of the moment it's different. If Davis pops up to left we're not talking about any of this. You make educated decisions and you move on."

When the questions came during the off-season, most focused on Game 7. Maddon defended himself, saying he stuck with the process he's always used; a pregame plan that only varied by a batter or two. He admitted his Game 6 mistake but wasn't budging on anything that happened the next day. And those questions continued long into the off-season. At charity banquets, baseball events, the winter meetings, and even the Cubs fan convention, Maddon was asked over and over again about those Game 7 decisions.

"It goes with the territory," he told ESPN.com in spring training of 2017. "If people want to criticize the way I managed Game 7, I'm okay with that. But I had a reason, a sound reason I believed, for everything I did in that game."

By the following spring, even players were getting tired of the second guessing.

"I felt bad for him," Lester said. "You just broke a 108-year curse and all off-season you had to sit there and answer questions about how you managed this game."

Not every player was onboard with his moves, of course. Right or wrong, nearly an entire bullpen was passed over in the series in favor of Chapman, while the lefty himself both offered his services but scoffed some at the overuse. In any case, the Cubs view it all as water under the bridge.

"If Guyer lines out to right field and we win that game 6–3, it's never an issue," Hoyer said. "I do think that that's the nature of baseball. The manager makes a lot of different decisions, and when he puts Travis Wood in left field [earlier in the season] and he makes a great catch, he looks like a genius. If that ball tips off his glove, it doesn't look quite as good. So, that's how I see it. I certainly think that with time people will remember him for the first two years as a Cubs manager—won 200 games and won a World Series. It doesn't get better than that."

Epilogue
2017

IMAGINE ACHIEVING YOUR LIFE'S DREAM. IMAGINE CLIMBING A mountain to reach its peak or running and finishing that marathon after years of training or just completing graduate school after a grueling course study, and imagine the whole world is watching as you do it.

Now imagine doing it all over again just three months later.

It's the scenario which faced Joe Maddon in 2017 after his Cubs broke the longest championship drought in professional sports history. After the parties and parades, along with the talk show appearances—and there were many of those as well—Maddon's task was to gather his team just 104 days later and ask them to achieve something no National League team has accomplished since 1975 and 1976: repeat as world champions.

If winning a World Series title with the Cubs is the greatest sports achievement in modern history, then what is winning it back-to-back years? Let's start with "extremely difficult." Even just returning to the World Series—or even the post-season—isn't exactly a sure thing in recent times. Due to the late end to the 2016 season combined with the World Baseball Classic playing its tournament early in 2017, spring training was upon the Cubs quicker than any in baseball history. The time off flew by, stacking the odds against the Cubs, no matter the talent and youth they possessed. There's a saying in sports that would ring true for the Cubs in 2017: staying on top can be every bit, if not more difficult, than getting there. And if they thought they had a target on their back in 2016, then imagine what it would be the following season. Teams were going to love beating the Cubs.

In many ways, Maddon might be the perfect manager for a baseball team attempting to repeat as champions, especially after a very short off-season. It's no secret the season is a grind, even more so with extra rounds of playoffs compared to year's past. Adding the World Baseball Classic to the schedule only made it longer, though infielder Javy Baez and pitcher Hector Rondon would be the only Cubs participants in the tournament. Maddon's biggest challenge in 2017 wouldn't be the opponent across the diamond as much as the mental and physical fatigue that accompanied winning it all in 2016. In other words, he'd have to deal with the "hangover" which has plagued championship teams in every sport.

But as documented over and over again in Maddon's career— especially with the Rays and Cubs—he already was a believer in rest over extra work. If anyone knew how to back off his players, allowing them some energy for later in the season, it was Maddon. The physical breaks came easy for him. We know he rested players more than most in plenty of years after not winning the World Series. Taking that to another level in 2017 wasn't going to be an issue. The bigger task, at least initially, was the mental aspect. How could the Cubs get up for spring games or even April ones after their adrenaline-filled run in 2016? Early in 2017, even before spring training began, Maddon began his messaging through the media.

"I want us to be uncomfortable," he said. "The moment you get into your comfort zone after having such a significant moment in your life like that, the threat is that you're going to stop growing.

"A mind once stretched has a very difficult time going back to its original form."

In other words, Maddon didn't want his players rolling into spring training with a satisfied air about them. By February and March, the previous year was supposed to be forgotten. That's easier said than done when it's the Chicago Cubs, a season after winning their first championship in 108 years. But Maddon tried nonetheless. "Uncomfortable" was one word he stressed. He had others.

"I'm really rotating around the thought of authenticity," Maddon stated just before the Cubs annual winter convention. "I talked about it a lot last year. Authenticity has a chance to repeat itself without even trying. It's part of who you are. It's not fabricated. It's real. I think one of our strongest qualities is the authentic component of our players. I'm focusing on that word right now."

This sort of mental messaging continued into spring training 2017.

"It's really important to become uncomfortable," Maddon continued. "If you become comfortable, that subtracts growth from the equation. I think if you remain uncomfortable, you continue to grow, you don't become stagnant or complacent. On every level, I want us to be uncomfortable, and I think that's a really positive word."

Who knows what made an impact for players, but there's little doubt once spring training began the Cubs were experiencing the hangover effect of playing into November in 2016. Where 2016 felt like a continuation of 2015, there was no "picking up where they left off" feeling in 2017. The Cubs would need time to recover, despite Maddon's messaging attempts. Maddon felt it too. His team wasn't exactly primed for April 2017, but they survived it. In fact, April felt like another month of spring training, especially on the mound, where the starting staff was nowhere near ready for prime time.

Knowing all they were up against, the Cubs 13–11 record in April 2017 wasn't all that bad. They were in first place in a division which didn't possess a great team. That would prove fortunate for Maddon as once he realized the situation at hand, he thought of two things he really wanted to stress: buying time and coming together as a team after adversity. The former came in the form of resting players and pulling starters early during a half where the Cubs weren't going to go on a run anyway. Instead of pressing the issue, Maddon did the opposite—as he often does. He backed off his players at a time where many would be pushing them. And he hoped the locker room would come together through it all.

"I believe that chemistry can create winning," Maddon said. "To really emphasize how important it's been to us over the last couple of years that the room itself has been such a big part of that. That we continue to stay together as a group and that as we do, the answers will come out of the room itself."

The adversity in 2017 would come in many forms. After leadoff-man Dexter Fowler signed with the St. Louis Cardinals in the off-season, the Cubs handed that job over to left-fielder Kyle Schwarber. It was a colossal failure, as the formerly injured Schwarber would end up in the minors after an awful start to the season. The Cubs admitted they overestimated Schwarber's abilities after missing nearly an entire season to a knee injury.

"The overreaction on my part was the fact that I didn't take into consideration enough that he didn't even play last year," Maddon said.

New injuries became the norm—perhaps also due to the short recovery period during the winter—and the Cubs languished in second place behind the Milwaukee Brewers for most of the first half. It was during these times that Maddon was actually at his best.

A potential low point came in June, when the Cubs were depleted to the point of fielding the youngest lineup for a World Series champion since 1997. They were in Washington, where the Nationals had championship aspirations of their own. Cubs' catcher Miguel Montero, a 2016 postseason hero, would be released during the series for speaking poorly about a teammate. Maddon seemingly had a lot working against him, but the Cubs split the four-game series. They were surviving with so much working against them. Soon, things would start to go their way. They just had to get to the All-Star Break.

"I know we haven't played our best but I look at that as a positive," Maddon said. "Geography has allowed us to stay in this. Now we're getting healthy."

He was referring to the Central Division of the National League. The Cubs were fortunate not to go up against the Nationals and Los Angeles Dodgers in order to return to the postseason. They only had to catch the Brewers, who were 5.5 games ahead of them at the break. That's when Maddon pushed the buttons which would vault them into first place.

The Cubs came out of the All-Star Break on fire, though Maddon continued to manage for the long run and not just the moment. The sense of urgency had returned, as did the adrenaline of a pennant race. As usual, Maddon didn't waver from his strategy of less is more. Again, he had a successful August (17–12)—and American Legion week—improving his record in that month since 2009 to 147–103. In the process, the Cubs took over first place for good, as one moment in September screamed Joe Maddon.

It was September 19. The Cubs were in Tampa Bay, playing against the Rays after an off-day. The division wasn't yet wrapped up, but MVP Kris Bryant wasn't in the lineup. He was healthy but Maddon gave him a second consecutive day off, sensing he was little fatigued. What manager would sit one of his best players after an off-day, during a pennant race? There may only be one. Over the final 10 games of the season, Bryant hit .375 with a 1.113 OPS, producing a microcosm for 2017. When things looked bleak, Maddon backed off, allowing his players time to find their game again. Eventually they did, and the Cubs won the division by 3.5 games.

The 2017 playoffs would be a grind of its own. The Cubs won a hard fought five-game series with the Nationals, leaving them with little left in the tank for the Dodgers. They succumbed easily in five games, but it didn't diminish what the team did in the regular season.

A World Series victory and three consecutive playoff appearances as manager of the Cubs has Maddon a step closer to the Hall of Fame. He's now reached the postseason in seven of his last 10 years in the dugout in two different cities. Trying not to suck has worked out pretty well for the former catcher who never made it to the big leagues as a player. He's made up for it as a manager, one who may go down as the most successful skipper ever, for two different franchises.

Sources

The (Wilkes-Barre, Pennsylvania) *Times Leader*
The (Allentown, Pennsylvania) *Morning Call*
Hazleton Standard-Speaker
The Tampa Tribune
The (Doylestown, Pennsylvania) *Intelligencer*
The (Easton) *Express-Times*
ESPN the Magazine
The Lafayette Magazine
The Tampa Bay Times
The Sporting News
Orange County Register
The Dallas Morning News
Long Beach Press-Telegram
The (Riverside, California) *Press Enterprise*
Philadelphia Inquirer
Worcester Telegram & Gazette (Massachusetts)
MLB.com
Sports Illustarted
The New York Times
Inland Valley Daily Bulletin (Ontario, California)

Interviews:
Joe Maddon, March 2007
Joe Maddon, February 2008
Joe Maddon, December 2007
Troy Percival, January 2017
Chuck Hernandez, January 2017
Kelly Shoppach, January 2017
Carlos Pena, January 2017
Vance Lovelace, January 2017
Randy Choate, February 2017
Joey Urso, February 2017
James Shields, January 2017
Gary DiSarcina, March 2017
David Price, March 2007
Rex Hudler, January 2007
Mike Scioscia, June 2010
Marc Topkin, March 2017
Roger Mooney, March 2017
Alex Cobb, March 2017
Evan Longoria, February 2017